I Can Read!

◆ **Write a word or number to finish each sentence.**

1. My name is ___Mason___ .

2. I am ___7___ years old.

3. I have ___0___ brothers.

4. I have ___1___ sisters.

5. I can ___read___ this book!

◆ **Draw a picture of your family.**

At the Park

◆ Look at the picture. Write how many of each you see.

1. swings

6
SIX

2. seesaws

3
three

3. slides

1
one

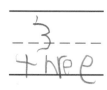

4. benches

2
two

◆ Underline the one that has more.

5.

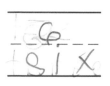

<u>swings</u>   or   benches

6.

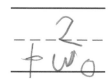

<u>benches</u>   or   slides

7.

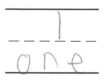

slides   or   <u>seesaws</u>

8.

seesaws   or   <u>swings</u>

Picture Clues/Comparing

Fun Literacy Activities for After-School Programs

Books & Beyond

by

**Sue Edwards
& Kathleen Martinez**

Illustrations by Mark Edwards

School-Age NOTES ● Nashville, Tennessee

About the Authors:

Sue Edwards, M. Ed. has been a family childcare provider, child development center program director and an accreditation endorser. Currently, Sue works as a project consultant and trainer for the California School-Age Consortium. Sue and her family live in Petaluma, California.

Kathleen Martinez, Ph.D. has been a remedial reading teacher, university professor and director of community-based resources for severely emotionally disturbed children and their families. She presently works as a consultant and trainer for after-school programs in the San Francisco Bay Area. She lives in Berkeley, California.

About the Illustrator:

Mark Edwards teaches art to children in the public school system, paints portraits, and is a freelance artist. Mark attended the Academy of Art in San Francisco and has received numerous awards for his art from various organizations.

ISBN: 0-917505-17-4

10 9 8 7 6 5 4 3 2 1

Published by School-Age NOTES, P.O. Box 40205, Nashville TN 37204-0205

Dedications

We thank and appreciate the people who helped us test drive all the activities in this book. Some of these people include the staff of Riverview Middle School, Bay Point, CA.; the staff and children at Ygnacio Valley Elementary School, Concord, CA; Miss Sara, Waugh Kids Care, Petaluma, CA; Sydney Moy, librarian extraordinaire, Meadow School, Petaluma, CA; East Bay Conservation Corps Tag Team, Oakland, CA; St. John's Threshold Center, San Francisco; various San Francisco after-school programs and all the other people who gave us feedback, encouragement and inspiration during various trainings.

Kathleen Martinez: To my friends for their encouragement and to my mom and dad and children for their support. Without their cheerleading and financial help this book would never have been written. To my fellow author, Sue Edwards, for keeping me on track and helping me reach my goals.

Sue Edwards: The heart of my every inspiration – Christopher, Candace and Zachary – you each provide me with all the love, support and encouragement I will ever need. I am here to provide you with the same, forever! Kathleen Martinez – thank you for making it a reality and for all your patience and martinis! Mark – you are much appreciated and loved.

Mark Edwards: To my wife, Sue, for the opportunity to have my dream come true. Christopher, Candace and Zachary, I love you very much.

Table of Contents

Activities for 11 – 14 year olds: Independent Readers

Integrating Literacy Development into After-School Programs

"Education is a social process; education is growth; education is not a preparation for life but is life itself."

John Dewey

Sitting in rows, children are making puppets of the characters in the story they have just read. Two middle-school boys work together on a script for their upcoming play. An eight-year old girl works with a mentor to sound out an unfamiliar word. Three adolescents write a letter to the local restaurant requesting a donated meal for the upcoming fundraiser. All these activities are common enough in our schools today. However, more frequently, these scenes are also taking place in after-school programs as these programs take on a larger role in the literacy development of young people. Many after-school programs have traditionally been involved in such efforts through tutoring and mentoring programs, homework assistance as well as sponsoring book clubs, reading corners and libraries. They engage participants in literacy activities as a part of their everyday practices often without being consciously aware that they are doing so. But, pressure is increasing to expand and become intentional in that involvement. This push is coming from many different directions. As funding for after-school programs increasingly flows through school districts, the schools are in a position to demand that these programs become involved in their agenda – academic achievement. Many foundations require that organizations address academic issues as

part of their grant proposals. After-school program staff recognize that young people need added support in developing essential literacy skills. For all these reasons, out-of-school staff are looking for ways to increase their capabilities in supporting literacy and still stay faithful to their unique mission of being something other than "more school."

Role of After-School Programs in Literacy Development

✎ To reinforce individual literacy skills

✎ To provide experiences that develop concepts and vocabulary

✎ To provide opportunities to apply literacy skills in new and practical ways

✎ To provide fun and engaging activities in which children use literacy skills in non-intimidating ways

✎ To provide opportunities for children to learn to enjoy books, writing and playing with language

Remember after-school programs are in a unique position to support literacy development in a variety of enriching ways. After-school programs do not have to imitate the school day to successfully integrate literacy into their program.

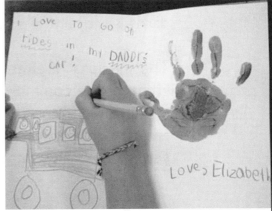

Similarities and Differences Between Schools and After-School Programs Affecting Approaches to Language Development

✎ **The goal of both school and after-school is to support young people in the development of their language literacy skills.**

The goal of school is to support the development of children's literacy in a direct instructional manner. Most schools approach that goal through the development of the academic skills of the children and by directly instructing the children in reading. Part of the goal of schools is reflected in their accountability for meeting academic standards.

After-school programs are not held to the same degree of accountability for helping children meet academic standards. However, they also have the goal of literacy development by providing skill reiniforcement and also by providing opportunities for children to use the skills in new and practical ways.

✎ **The specific mission of schools and after-school programs are usually different.**

The mission of school is to educate in academics. Although the way schools approach that mission varies a great deal from school to school, the development of academic skills usually as defined by state standards is the central focus of their work.

The missions of after-school programs vary extensively. Some programs have a commitment to recreational activities. Others focus on the encouragement of the arts. Others work to increase leadership and service opportunities for the youth involved. Still others see themselves specifically supporting and extending the school mission.

✎ Attendance in school and in after-school programs affects the kinds of activities that can be planned.

Attendance in school is mandatory. Usually you can count on children being there. Therefore, long-term projects can be planned and carried out over a series of days. You can develop skills sequentially over a long period of time.

Participation in after-school programs is usually voluntary. Activities must attract the participants by their quality and fun. Attendance is often sporadic. When planning activities, it is not always possible to count on the same participants being there more than one day in a row or the same number of hours per day.

✎ The difference in the way space is allocated affects the kind of activities that can be planned.

In school, the teachers can usually count on a self-contained space where they can keep materials up and display children's work over a period of time. There is space for quiet work and also group work. The teacher usually has control over the environment of the classroom.

In after-school programs, the staff often has to share space with other programs or has limited space. There is less of an opportunity to keep projects displayed and often materials have to be carted and repacked after every session. The after-school staff often has to be creative in how they set up the space for their programs.

Purpose of this Book

This book will:

✎ Provide fun and easily prepared enrichment activities that integrate literacy for children ranging in ages from five to fourteen, with varying literacy skill level from emergent to independent reading ability.

✎ Help program staff develop "intentionality" in the process of language development.

✎ Provide program staff with language to communicate how the activities the children are engaged in support literacy development; and

✎ Provide materials and lists of resources to support continued literacy development in the after-school program.

This book will not:

✎ Will not provide methods for direct instruction of literacy skills;

✎ Will not discuss one-on-one tutoring of children in after-school programs; or

✎ Will not provide a complete literacy curriculum for after-school programs.

After-school programs already do many things that support literacy development. We hope that this book will provide exciting new ideas to enrich your programs.

Frequently Asked Questions: Language Literacy Development for After-School Programs

What is Language Literacy?

A "literate" person, a person who can read, walks into your program and sees the following poster:

They might be thinking, "What in the world is the poster trying to say? The symbols seem to be organized like words. There is some punctuation and what seems to be a capital letter at the beginning. But what does it mean?"

An English reader walks into your program and sees the following poster:

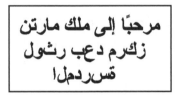

She might recognize that the symbols represent some kind of language – in this case Arabic – but has no way of decoding its meaning. She cannot **read** it.

Another individual who can read English walks into your program and see the following sign:

> **Welcome to the**
> **Martin Luther King Jr.**
> **After-School**
> **Learning Center**

Instantly he understands what is being communicated, because he can make meaning out of the symbols. However, a child who cannot read walks into your program and sees the sign, has the same experience of the previous two people. She might recognize some of the letters, but has no idea what the words are and what they mean. In reality, for the child, the sign is as meaning-less as the second sign is for the English reader.

Basically, then, language literacy involves **the ability to make meaning out of sound symbols** when *speaking and listening* and **written symbols** when *reading and writing*. A "literate" person understands the symbols fluently and usually automatically. However, we had to learn how to make meaning out of what is basically an arbitrary system of both written and sound symbols.

> **The process of learning how to use a basically arbitrary sound-symbol system is what we mean by language literacy development.**

What are the Elements of Language Literacy?

Language literacy encompasses the use of all the different forms of language that has meaning and which we use to make meaning. We make sense of and use language when we

- ✎ **Read**

- ✎ **Write**

- ✎ **Speak**

- ✎ **Listen**

There is a reason why educational standards talk about "language arts," rather than "reading, spelling, etc." These forms of language use are interrelated and difficult to separate. In order to speak, we have to hear language first. If you have seen the movie, "The Miracle Worker," you might remember that Helen Keller had to connect a "word" to a concept, in order to understand language. Her breakthrough in language came about when she recognized that "water" was connected to the liquid coming out of the tap. Only then did her language development take off. In order to write, we need to be able to read except if we are copying, which is not really "writing," since we might not be able to understand what we are copying. Until we become very sophisticated in our reading ability, we need to have the concepts and the vocabulary in our spoken language in order to understand what we are reading. All the different language modes are interrelated.

What is Meant By Being Literate?

> **Literacy is the ability to use language in all its forms fluently and in a way that allows one to use language to function effectively in society.**

In order to be literate, we have had to master with a high level of fluency, the skills of

Breaking the language code,
Comprehending what is written or heard,
Critiquing and evaluating,
Applying, and
Using language conventions.

More specifically, the skills that we use in these categories include the following:

a. We break the language code through
1. *Word and sound analysis*
2. *Sight word recognition*
3. *Understanding the vocabulary and concepts being used*
4. *Understanding the concept of print*

b. We comprehend what is written or heard by
1. *Identifying details*
2. *Identifying elements of a story grammar/map – characters, setting, plot*
3. *Identifying main ideas and supporting details*
4. *Identifying the sequence of a story*
5. *Comparing and contrasting*
6. *Inferring outcomes and information*

c. We critique and evaluate by
1. *Distinguishing between different literary genres*
2. *Evaluating the author's use of various techniques*
3. *Critiquing the credibility, adequacy, accuracy, and appropriateness of what is read*

d. We use language conventions in
1. *Organization*
2. *Penmanship*
3. *Spelling*
4. *Punctuation*
5. *Grammar*

e. We apply the skills of literacy when we
1. *Write and tell narratives, persuasive arguments, reports, summaries etc.*
2. *Read and research for information*
3. *Read and write for enjoyment*

This is not an exhaustive list of the various skills involved in literacy, but provides a good starting point for thinking about what is required in order to develop comprehension. We often talk about comprehension as the ability to read "the lines, between the lines, and past the lines." The glossary at the back of the book provides definitions of some of the skills listed above.

What Can You Expect at Different Developmental Stages and at Different Grade Levels in Regard to Literacy Development?

The research indicates that everyone, regardless of age, goes through the following stages of literacy development. When working in after-school programs, many of the participants have not mastered the skills of the previous stage. We strive to provide experiences that will help them gain those skills in fun non-instructional ways.

Emergent Reader : Typically Kindergarten – Early First Grade

The child will:

- Seek out and enjoy experiences with books and other print material
- Recognize their names in print and be able to write them
- Talk about experiences and discoveries
- Write letters, lower and upper case
- Begin to understand the relationship between letters and sounds: Alphabet sequence, letter recognition, beginning sounds
- Play with rhyming and become aware of syllables
- Develop basic comprehension strategies: know the main idea and can recall details
- Understand the basic plot and sequence of simple stories
- Begin to acquire early sight word vocabulary

In early stages of learning to write, children will pretend to write, using wavy scribbles or "nonsense" symbols. They will begin to attempt to form letters and use invented spelling. Gradually they will begin to string letters together, but they will have trouble with spacing letters and words. They might represent whole words with beginning letters or consonants. They will begin to write entire words, especially their names and other sight words.

Initial Reader : Typically second half of the 1st grade – 2nd grade

The child will:

- Demonstrate increased motivation to read for pleasure and information
- Figure out unknown words using a variety of strategies, including picture clues, knowledge of word structure and letter-sound relationships
- Decode many unfamiliar words by identifying sound-symbol relationships, (i.e. blends, digraphs, vowel sounds)
- Recognize and use clues within the text (e.g., sentence structure, word meaning, punctuation), rereading and other strategies as aids in developing fluency and comprehension

- Make and confirm predictions about what will be found in a text and draw logical conclusions
- Write complete sentences and eventually simple paragraphs
- Recognize and use repeated readings as an aid to developing fluency and understanding appropriate materials
- Develop more extensive sight word vocabulary
- Distinguish between fiction and nonfiction

Children will use more conventional patterns in their spelling and the form of their writing. They will continue to become more fluent and sophisticated in their use of standard spelling. The organization of their writing will also become increasingly sophisticated and fluent.

Transitional Reader: Typically 2ⁿᵈ grade through 3ʳᵈ grade

The child will:
- Demonstrate an understanding that reading is a way to gain information
- Develop more advanced knowledge of complex patterns (e.g., prefixes, suffixes, chunks)
- Identify more complex story elements (e.g., beginning, middle and end, plot, setting, characters, problem/solution)
- Understand the main idea of simple nonfiction materials
- Rely heavily on letter/sound knowledge to read text
- Develop combination of decoding and comprehension strategies
- Develop more sophisticated comprehension strategies
- Continue to enlarge sight word vocabulary and speaking/writing vocabulary
- Respond to speakers by listening attentively, and commenting and questioning appropriately
- Begin to write cursive
- Gain more sophistication in writing

Independent Reader: Continue to gain greater and greater fluency throughout life

The child will:
- Select and read a variety of narrative and informative texts independently and fluently
- Recognize why a text is written and use the appropriate strategies to aid comprehension
- Determine the meaning, pronunciation, and use of unknown words by using a dictionary
- Continue to enlarge reading, oral and writing vocabulary
- Demonstrate an understanding of sentence structure
- Respond in oral and written form to a variety of texts (e.g., ask questions, cite supporting passages, compare to other readings and life experiences)
- Identify main characters, plot, setting, important details, and recurring themes in literature
- Identify dialogue, nonverbal cues, points of view, and author's purpose
- Use various informational parts of a text (e.g., chapter and section headings, index, table of contents, glossary, appendices)

- Use key comprehension strategies (e.g., access prior knowledge, identify purpose, identify and summarize main idea, connect new information)
- Use print and non-print resources (e.g., encyclopedias, dictionaries, trade books, people, indexes, technology)
- Make observations about the use of language, graphic symbols, and idioms in various contexts

What Can We Do in the After-School Program to Help Children Develop Their Literacy Abilities?

The after-school programs have greater flexibility and can provide more opportunities for enrichment activities. Therefore, in after-school programs, the participants can gain greater

✎ **Opportunities to use literacy skills in real life situations**

✎ **Opportunities to practice literacy skills**

✎ **Opportunities to have fun with literacy skills**

✎ **Opportunities to be exposed to new concepts and experiences.**

After-school programs do not have to become more like school to help their participants in literacy development. We have a unique opportunity and responsibility to support literacy development in new and creative ways. A definition of craziness is doing the same thing over and over and expecting a different result. Let us not be crazy in our after-school programs. Let us approach literacy development in a different way, so we have a chance of getting different results.

Overview of Activities & Structure of Book

✎ The activities are divided by age level. However, with minimal modifications most of the activities can be used and enjoyed by all ages. **Check out all the activities to see if your participants would enjoy them regardless of the suggested age.**

✎ The activities in each section are in alphabetical order.

✎ The activities can be used independently or integrated into enrichment programs. In each age level section, there are four activities that can easily be integrated into the following enrichment areas:

> **Science**
> **Arts and Crafts**
> **Games/Community Service**
> **Literature and Creative Writing**
> **Drama**
> **Movement and Dance**

✎ Each activity includes the following components:

Staff Role and Space: Provides a general description of the role of the staff and space required for doing the activity.

Materials: Lists both the necessary and optional materials needed to successfully complete the activity.

Time: The prep and minimum times listed are merely approximations. Modify or extend the activities to fit your program needs.

Adaptations/Modifications: The sections are divided by age level. However, most of the activities can be done and would be of interest to any age child. Check out the adaptation/modification area in each section to see how you can change it to use with older and younger children.

Directions: Step-by-step directions on how to do the activity to get the greatest literacy development benefit.

Extensions: Ideas that you can use to expand the activity.

Content Standards: The standards statements are based on the California State Reading/Language Arts Content Standards. Most states use similar language. The intent of this section is to help after-school providers discuss with parents and school personnel how their program activities support academic skills development.

Suggested Resources: Names of books and stories that can be used in the activity or can be used to supplement the activity. The complete publication information is listed in the back of the book.

Hints for Getting the Most Literacy Development Out of the Activities

✎ **Surround the participants with the written word.** Signs, posters, books, all kinds of writing, especially examples of participants' writing should be all over the program area. Many programs share space and can not leave material up. Look for ways to show participants' works such as portable display boards or a display case that has been designated by the site.

✎ **Provide many samples of completed projects** so the participants have new ideas on how to approach the activities. If the young people want to take their projects home, you can take pictures or make copies of projects.

✎ **Always be aware of the literacy component of the activities.** Some of the activities, especially the arts and crafts and science ones could be done without integrating the literacy skills. Stay intentional!

✎ **Write the words.** Before you ask participants to write anything, brainstorm vocabulary words with the whole group. Write the words on chart paper or a board. This will increase both the quantity and quality of their writing.

✎ **Keep questions open-ended.** When you are discussing books, ideas for writing, or plans for doing projects with the participants, make sure to keep questions open-ended. Ask yourself, "Does this question have a yes or no answer?" If it does, re-word the questions so that the participants will have to give a thoughtful response.

✎ **Be open to the creativity of the participants.** In other settings, such as school, participants are often required to write or complete assignments in very specific ways in order to demonstrate that they have mastered a skill. One of the advantages of the after-school program is that the staff and the participants are not limited in this way. After-school programs are a place where the participants can experiment and try out their own voices.

✎ **Keep the audience in mind.** If you want the children to rewrite or take care with the projects, have an audience in mind for the final product. Have an art or drama show. Have them make the product for their families. Give the projects a purpose.

Activities for Children
Ages Five Through Eight
Emergent, Initial & Transitional Readers

1. The activities match the developmental needs of the age of the children because each activity

   - Does not take a lot of time to finish,
   - Can be done individually,
   - Does not result in a complicated end product, and
   - Is focused on ideas that directly affect the children's immediate lives.

2. The activities match the reading, writing and speaking ability of most children at this age. At this age most children are at one of the following stages of literacy development:

   - **Emergent:** They are becoming aware of books, letters and sound. They cannot read or write anything independently.

   - **Initial:** They are able to read and write simple words and books with help. They are beginning to learn how to decode new words but cannot do it independently.

   - **Transitional:** They are able to read simple books and write simple narratives and descriptions.

Unit Ideas

Many of the activities can be used as the basis of a long-term unit or club. Check out the extension ideas for more ideas on how to extend the project into a unit. For example:

   - **Insect Unit:** *Creature Feature*
   - **Autobiography Unit:** *Name Poems, It's All About Me* and *Hey, That's Me*
   - **Food Unit:** *What's For Lunch?*
   - **Movie Unit:** *Storyboarding*

Act It Out Memory

Staff Role and Space

Staff will provide instruction and supervision.
Table space and chairs

Time

Prep Time: 30 minutes to make cards
Minimum Time Needed:
45-minute session

Supplies

Twenty-four Drama Memory Cards made with 3 x 5 index cards (directions included)

Adaptation/Modifications

✎ Add pictures to cards for children who are not fluent readers.
✎ Encourage children to use facial expressions instead of solely large gestures.

Purpose

For children to practice sight word recognition, develop memory and concentration skills while performing and having a fun time.

Directions

Making the Drama Memory Cards

1. Like the regular Memory game, you will need two sets of identical cards. Each set will consist of 12 cards, 24 cards total.

2. Write simple actions to act out on cards. You will need 12 different actions – see suggestions that follow. Be creative with your actions!

Acting it Out

1. Shuffle the cards and place them face down in an orderly arrangement.

2. Two children at a time play. Taking turns, each child turns over one card at a time and acts out the action on the card. After acting out the first card, a second card is chosen and acted out.

3. If the two cards match, the child picks them both up and places them to the side. This child chooses two more cards and acts them out.

4. The children continue taking turns choosing cards and acting them out until all cards have been matched up.

5. The winner is the child with the most matching pairs after all cards have been matched up.

Psst...
This is a fabulous circle time activity to play with energetic small groups.

Suggestions for Simple Actions

- ✎ Be a kitty cat
- ✎ Fly like a plane
- ✎ Blow like a tree in the wind
- ✎ Open like a flower
- ✎ Be a clown in the circus
- ✎ Drive a bus
- ✎ Dance
- ✎ You are Spiderman
- ✎ Become a princess
- ✎ Ride a horse
- ✎ Swim
- ✎ Walk a tight rope

Extension Ideas

✎ Have the children make more elaborate cards that require more drama skills.

✎ Play Human Drama Memory (See Feelings List reproducible found on page 173.)

- Children stand in rows
- Pairs of feelings are assigned to the children.
- Two children stand out of the rows and choose the children as if they were cards.
- When chosen, the children act out their feeling.
- When a match is made, the matching two children move out. Points are given per match, just like the card game.

"Content Standards"

Reading

Concepts About Print

✎ Understand that printed materials provide information.

✎ Read simple one-syllable and high-frequency words.

Reproducibles on p. 173 & 175

Bark Writing

Staff Role and Space

Staff should give initial directions and provide support and supervision.
Can be done in any space, but best if participants can work at tables.

Time

Prep Time: Minimal
Minimum Time Needed:
        Two 45-minute sessions
(Best if the paper is allowed to dry overnight.)

Supplies

Brown paper bags
Crayons
Black tea (enough to soak the paper)
Scrap paper
Pencils
Black chalk (optional)

Adaptation/Modifications

✎ Children can also make pictographs instead of words to illustrate the message.
✎ For younger children who can not write, have them dictate the story to a staff member who will write it on a sheet of paper, and then have the children copy it on the "bark" paper.
✎ Have the children brainstorm words that they might write in a message calling for help. Write the words on chart paper so they can use them in their messages.

Purpose

To encourage creative writing.

Directions

1. Set the stage for the activity by telling the children the following:

> Pretend that you are traveling through a forest and you do not have any paper. You want to send a message back home, but have nothing to write on. You remember that early people once used bark. So you decide to write on "bark."

2. Talk to the children that since it would be harmful to trees to use actual bark, they are going to make pretend bark for their messages.

3. Take a brown grocery bag and cut out a large piece, or rip out a large piece for a more natural look.

4. Thoroughly soak the paper in black tea, but not enough to make it disintegrate.

5. Crumple up the piece of brown paper as if you were making a ball.

6. Carefully smooth it out and let it dry overnight. It will look similar to bark the next day. To make it look really old, rub black chalk around the edges. This gives the paper a distinctive antique look.

7. Brainstorm different words that they might use in their messages such as <beautiful trees>, <hungry>, <happy.> Write these words on a board or chart paper so that the children can refer to them when they are writing.

> Psst...
> Setting the stage for writing is critical. The more you get them to talk about ideas they can include in their writing, the richer their writing will be.

8. While the paper bag is drying, have the children write a draft of their message on a piece of paper. Staff should help with spelling.

9. When the brown paper is dry, have the children copy the message with crayons, and then decorate the paper with pictures that illustrate it.

Suggested Resources
✎ *Papermaking for Kids: Simple Steps to Handcrafted Paper*, **Beth Wilkinson**, for detailed directions for making paper.

✎ See the suggested website in the back of the book for directions on making paper.

Extension Ideas
✎ Use this activity as part of a unit including "Hug a Tree." They can use their bark paper for writing their tree description.

✎ Have a unit on paper making. See the suggested resources for other paper making activities.

✎ Show examples of Bark Painting from Australia. Have the children paint one on their paper bark.

✎ For 4th and 5th grade children, read the book "My Side of the Mountain" by Jean Craighead George. There are many ideas for survival strategies that the children can build and try.

"Content Standards"
Writing Strategies
Organization and Focus
✎ Select a focus when writing.
✎ Use descriptive words when writing.
Penmanship
✎ Create readable documents with legible handwriting.
Evaluation and Revision
✎ Revise original drafts to improve sequence and provide more descriptive detail.
Writing Applications
✎ Write brief narratives based on their experiences.

Bookmarks

Staff Role and Space

Staff will give directions and support and supervise activity. For younger children, they will also have to prepare template in advance.

Your daily art activity center works great.

Time

Prep Time: Gathering of materials and making the templates: 45 minutes

Minimum Time Needed:
  45-minute session

Supplies

Construction paper
Markers and crayons
Scissors
Yarn
Contact paper, or laminator
Stickers, magazines to cut, etc.
Glitter and imagination!

Adaptation/Modifications

✎ Older children can help younger children with spelling and writing.

✎ Encourage children to write in their home language.

Purpose

To encourage love of reading by involving children in creative activities related to books, and to reinforce concepts about print.

Directions

1. Before children start their bookmarks, have them look at various picture books. While children are looking, discuss their favorite books and authors. Have them choose one book they will use as the theme for their bookmark.

2. Cut out template, 8" x 2", for a standard bookmark. Older children may design shape, trace and cut out their own bookmarks.

3. Allow children to explore available supplies and decorate their bookmarks. They should include the title and the author on their bookmark.

4. Laminate or cover bookmarks with clear contact paper leaving a 1/2" edge on the top. Using a paper punch, punch a hole in the trim on the top edge and tie a ribbon or yarn through it.

5. Put the bookmarks to use! Show the children how to use them to mark their place while they are reading. They can also use it instead of their fingers to track the words.

Psst...
These make wonderful gifts for teachers, parents and friends.

Psst...
Have the children personalize their bookmarks with names of favorite authors, friends or book titles.

Extension Ideas

✎ Visit your local library or a bookstore and ask for samples of the free bookmarks they may distribute.

✎ Have the children take their bookmarks to a senior center.

✎ They can make their name (acrostic) poems on their bookmarks.

✎ When they do the activity "Dear Favorite," they can include a book-mark in their letter.

✎ Make an album or bulletin board of bookmarks representing the stories that the children have read.

✎ Use photographs!

✎ Write favorite quotes from books on the bookmarks.

✎ Include multicultural books in the selection that the children look at before making the bookmarks.

✎ Encourage the children to use their own language in decorating the bookmarks.

"Content Standards"
Reading
Concepts about Print
✎ Identify title and author of a reading selection.
Literary Response and Analysis
✎ Recollect, talk and write about books read during the school year.

5-8 year olds
Emergent, Initial & Transitional Readers
Older children will also enjoy!

Bottle Blues

Staff Role and Space

Adult will provide directions, write or supervise the writing of the numbers. Counter or table top space that is okay to get wet.

Time

Prep Time: Time for gathering bottles and making copies of the music
Minimum Time Needed:
    45-minute session

Supplies

Six drinking glasses or juice bottles
Snapple® bottles are a great size
Water
Masking tape
Wooden spoon or stick
Notebook and pencils

Purpose

To be able to follow directions and understand patterns. To increase phonemic awareness.

Directions

1. Fill six juice bottles with different amounts of water. The six different levels will make a six note scale.

2. Line the bottles up starting with the one with the most amount of water to the one with the least amount of water.

3. With the masking tape, label the bottles #1-#6. Number one has the most water, six has the least.

4. Assist children in playing the songs by tapping on the bottles with the wooden spoon or stick. Copy the music and post it on the wall near the bottles to help the children read the music on their own.

5. Keep a notebook and pencil nearby to encourage composing.

If you use bottles the size of Snapple® bottles, fill them as follows:

1	2	3	4	5	6
3"	2 1/2"	2"	1 1/2"	1"	1/2"

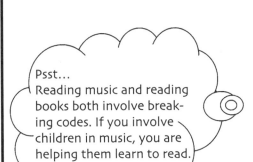

Psst...
Reading music and reading books both involve breaking codes. If you involve children in music, you are helping them learn to read.

Check it Out

Tapping the bottles with the stick causes the water to vibrate and produce a sound. The water dampens the vibrations. So, the less water, the higher the pitch!

Put the stick down and blow into the bottles of water. This causes the air to vibrate which causes the opposite effect! Now the bottles with the most amount of water produce the higher pitch!

The numbers to the songs represent the numbers on the bottles. Here are a few songs for you to play on your Bottle Blues:

Jingle Bells	**This Old Man**
333 333 35123	535 535 6543234
444 4433 3355421	345 1 111 12345

Twinkle, Twinkle Little Star
11 55 66 5 44 33 22 1
55 44 33 2 55 44 33 2
11 55 66 5 44 33 22 1

Extension Ideas

✎ Leave the bottles set up in your science activity area to encourage children to experiment.

✎ Use a keyboard, xylophone or any musical instrument to accompany the Bottle Blues.

✎ Encourage children to compose their own songs and write them down for others to try.

✎ Set the bottles up on a window ledge to catch the sun. This is especially interesting if you color the water.

✎ It is fun and visually appealing to add a few drops of different food coloring to the bottles. For instance, bottle #1 can be red, #2 blue, etc.

✎ Add two more bottles for a complete octave.

✎ Experiment with different amounts of bottles and water!

"Content Standards"
Reading
Concepts in Print
✎ Follow words from left to right.
Phonemic Awareness
✎ Track and represent the number, sameness/difference , and order of two and three isolated phonemes.
Listening
Comprehension
✎ Understand and follow one-and two step directions.

Character Cutouts

Staff Role and Space

Staff reads the story and leads discussion, then supervises and encourages.
Room for children to lay down on the floor.
Quiet Area for listening or reading

Time

Prep Time: Time to gather materials
Minimum Time Needed:
Two 45-minute sessions —
15 minutes to introduce the story and talk about characters
30 minutes to read the story
10 minutes to review the story and to talk about the characteristics of the characters
30 minutes to make and decorate the cutouts.

Supplies

- Story that includes strong characters
- Butcher paper/postal wrapping paper at least the length of your tallest participant
- Colored Markers/crayons/colored pencils
- Scissors

Adaptation/Modifications

- Older fluent readers can read the story to the participants.
- Match participants who can write better with those who have more difficulty.
- Before having the participants write the characteristics on their cutouts, the group could brainstorm vocabulary, and the staff member would write these words on the board or a chart paper, so the children can copy them on their cutouts.
- For older children, have them choose the books.

Purpose

To be able to describe and relate to characters in books.

Directions

1. Select a book with at least two strong characters. It could also be a short story.

2. Before reading the book, talk to the children about describing people. You might tell them to use questions like this:

- What do they look like? Color of their hair, how tall they are, etc.
- What are their personalities like? Are they friendly, mean, etc.
- What do they like or not like to do?
- How do they treat other people?
- What are some things they have done recently?
- Who are their family and their friends?

3. Have the children describe someone they know.

4. Bring the characters in the book to the attention of the children.

- Tell them that they are going to listen to a story that has some interesting characters in it.
- Give them the names of the characters.
- Tell them that they are going to describe these characters later.

5. As you read the story, occasionally ask them about the characters?

- What are they doing?
- How are they feeling?
- How are they acting?

Psst…
Remember to select books that have multicultural characters so that all participants can identify with them.

6. After you have finished the story, have the children break into pairs and have each pair choose a character from the book.

7. Help the children make their cutouts.

✎ Roll out long sheets of paper, one for each child.

✎ Have the children take turns tracing each other's outline on the pieces of paper.

✎ Have them write or draw different things that describe their character inside the cutout figure.

8. After they have traced and filled in their outline, have them cut it out.

9. Encourage the children to color and decorate their Character Cutouts like the characters in the book.

Suggested Books

✎ *Grandma and Me at the Flea,* **Juan Felipe Herrera**

✎ *Bad Case of Stripes,* **David Shannon**

✎ *A Chair for my Mother,* **Vera Williams**

✎ *My Rotten Redheaded Older Brother,* **Patricia Polacco**

✎ *Jamaica Louise Jones,* **Amy Hest**

✎ *Luka's Quilt,* **Georgia Guback**

✎ *Frog and Toad are Friends,* **Arnold Lobel**

Extension Ideas

✎ Encourage more extensive decoration of the cut-out figures— adding yarn hair, etc.

✎ Make a portable mural by pasting the figures on large paper and drawing a picture of one of the scenes of the story as the background.

✎ Make large puppets out of the cutouts by gluing them on stiffer paper or cardboard. Attach a stick to the back that can be used to maneuver the figures.

✎ Make up plays using the puppet character cutouts to reenact scenes in the book.

✎ Make a life-size story board.

✎ Cut out two copies of the outline. Staple them together leaving an opening to stuff with newspaper to create a puffy cutout.

"Content Standards"
Reading
Narrative Text: Elements of a story
✎ Identifying characters
✎ Comparing and contrasting characters.
Vocabulary development
Listening and Speaking
✎ Retelling stories, using characters, plot and setting.

Chunky Chalk Hopscotch

Staff Role and Space

Adults supervision of children and assist in spelling as necessary.
Outdoor black top or cement ground

Time

Prep time: Time to gather supplies and to make the template
Minimum time needed:
    45-minute session

Supplies

✎ Large sidewalk chalk
✎ Small stones or beanbags for tossing.
✎ A square approximately 12x12 inches that the children can use to trace on the ground. A piece of cardboard works well.

Adaptation/Modifications

✎ For children who can not yet write their names, write their name very lightly and have them trace it boldly.
✎ Children who can not jump or hop may enjoy tossing a pebble or beanbag onto the different letters as they say them out loud.

Purpose

For children to practice letter recognition and also for a fun time!

Directions

1. Have the children write their names using the sidewalk chalk on the ground.

2. Have them count out the letters in their names.

3. Provide a traditional hopscotch design for the children to use as an example.

4. Assist children in tracing around the square template to produce a hopscotch plan specifically for their name! Instead of numbers, the children write the letters of their names in the large squares.

> For example, the name Candace will have 7 squares. The children can place the squares in any desirable shape as long as each square is connected.

5. As with traditional hopscotch, the children hop from square to square and say the letter they land on.

Psst...
Children with shorter first names may want to include their middle or last name initials to add to the hopscotch.

Traditional Hopscotch Rules

1. The first player tosses the pebble onto the first square.

2. They then hop over the first square and land on two feet on the second and third square, side by side.

3. They then hopscotch up to the last square, turn around and hopscotch back down.

4. When they come to the square right above the one with the pebble on it, they bend down and pick the pebble up and hop into that square.

5. The first player then tosses the pebble onto the second square and repeat process.

6. If you throw the pebble to a square and you miss, it is the other person's turn.

7. The winner is the first person to complete the game.

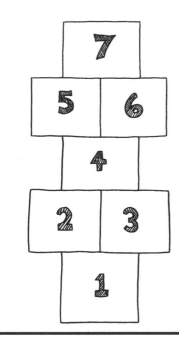

Extension Ideas

✎ Challenge children to make hopscotch plans with their first and last names.

✎ Jump rope silly sing-songs using the names of the children are a lot of fun!

✎ As a group project, challenge children to make a huge hopscotch with all the letters in the alphabet.

✎ Create a hopscotch board inside with masking tape to use on cold or wet days.

✎ The staff can write sight words or spelling words in the squares of a traditional hopscotch design and have the children say or spell the words while playing.

"Content Standards"
Reading
Decoding and word recognition
✎ Match all consonant and short vowel sounds to appropriate letters.
Writing Strategies
Penmanship
✎ Write upper case and lower case letters of the alphabet independently.
✎ Print legibly and space letters appropriately.

Creature Feature

Staff Role and Space

Staff will supervise children, initiate discussions and assist in writings.
An outdoor area to explore and dig.

Time

Prep Time: Gathering of the materials especially the jars needs to be done ahead of time because it might take a while.
Minimum Time Needed:
At least three 45-minute sessions
Session 1: Discussion and find bugs (make sure they put holes in the lid)
Session 2: Brainstorm the ideas for the graphic organizer and begin poster
Session 3: Finish poster

Supplies

Bug jars (These can be small jam jars with lids, or special jars bought from a distributor.)
Magnifying glasses
Poster boards or large construction paper
Pens, markers, pencils
Scrap paper
Science and nature magazines to cut up
Scissors
Glue
Rulers

Adaptation/Modification

✎ Fluent spellers can assist other children with proper spelling on scrap paper before final copy on poster.
✎ Children who can not write fluently yet, can just use pictures and orally describe their poster.
✎ Younger children may dictate their observations to an older child to write for them.
✎ This makes a great small group project. Everyone work together on one poster!

Purpose

To encourage observations and to write and organize descriptions and to provide opportunities for creative writing.

Directions

1. Discuss with children that they will be creating 'Creature Features'. These are posters all about the bugs that they have caught and observed. Have the children notice the following:
   ✎ where they caught the bugs,
   ✎ what surrounded the bug, and
   ✎ other living things in their environment.

2. Provide the children with their bug jars and out they go to explore and collect 'creatures', bugs!

3. After the bugs are caught, the children will create miniature habitats for their creatures. Leaves and dirt may be added to the jar to imitate the natural habitats where the bugs lived. Be sure to punch holes in the lids for air!

4. Provide children with scrap paper to make notes and observations about the environment where they caught the creatures.

5. Have them use the graphic organizer found on page 177 to brainstorm descriptions of the bug including
   ✎ color
   ✎ size
   ✎ length
   ✎ number of legs, etc.
   ✎ personality
   ✎ habitat

Psst…
Be aware, if an adult is viewed by the children as squeamish about bugs, the children may limit their own explorations. Be brave and show that bugs are cool!

Bug Mania

Featuring Beatles

They are hungry!

Soundtrack Available by The Beatles

Rated G

6. Have children create a rough draft of a poster featuring their bugs. Suggest a movie type poster, or a book cover. Check spelling on these rough drafts.

7. Next, the Creature Feature posters will be made to share facts and observations with others about the bugs. Using writing, magazine pictures and drawings, children will be creative and share all about their bugs on a poster.

8. Encourage children to title their poster clearly across the top center of the board. Creative names add fun and focus, such as 'Planet of the Ants'.

9. Movie poster samples and books may be shared with the children to encourage creativity. Stories focused on the life of a bug usually work well to focus Creature Feature posters.

10. When posters are complete, display them for parents and have children share!

11. Be sure to let bugs loose back where they were found outside!

Suggested Resources

Non-Fiction:

✎ *Entomology*, **Ellen Doris**

✎ *Fascinating World of Ants,* **Angels Julivert**

✎ *Eyewitness: Insect,* **Laurence Mound**

Fiction:

✎ Check out the fiction books by **Eric Carle** like *The Very Hunger Caterpillar*

Extension Ideas

✎ Instead of posters, have children write poems about their bugs.

✎ Share books about bugs and insects with the children.

✎ Daily journal writings about the life of a bug are a lot of fun!

✎ Use a movie camera to film short bug features!

✎ Watch a movie such as *"A Bug's Life"* and talk about whether the movie portrayed bugs accurately.

"Content Standards"

Reading

Vocabulary Development

✎ Classify grade appropriate categories of words.

Writing Strategies

✎ Use descriptive words when writing.

✎ Write descriptions that use concrete sensory details to present and support unified impressions of people, things or experiences.

Listening and Speaking

Comprehension

✎ Share information and ideas.

Reproducible on p. 177

Drumming Rhymes

Staff Role and Space

Staff will introduce activity to children. They will supervise and encourage the building of the drums, and then assist the children to beat their drums in rhythm of words.

An art or activity center with tables.

Time

Prep Time: Prep work will include gathering the coffee cans and cutting construction paper to fit around the cans

Minimum Time Needed:

45 minutes to create and decorate drums.

45 minutes to read rhymes and practice drumming.

Supplies

Coffee cans with plastic lids
Construction paper
Glue
Scissors
Markers
Dowels
Scrap materials including string, leather, feathers and beads

Adaptation/Modifications

✎ Children who have a difficult time with the rhythm will benefit from having an adult holding their hands and helping them drum a few times.

Purpose

To encourage children to become aware of the rhythm of language and syllable counts by reciting rhymes while enjoying music and crafts.

Directions

1. Gather children and explain that they will be making drums. These drums will be used to keep the beat to the rhymes you share.

2. Discuss the rhythm of rhymes, or the beat of the syllables. Practice keeping a beat to rhymes by having the children clap their hands to the rhythm.

3. Next, provide children with materials to make drums. Have the construction paper cut the right size to wrap around the cans.

4. Encourage the children to draw designs and creatures on the construction paper. You may also have them write their favorite rhyme on the construction paper.

5. Next, wrap and glue the decorated paper around the can. Glue additional decorations, such as feathers, etc., to the can. When glue is dry, place lids on cans.

6. When they finish their drums, join the children together and have them practice their drumming. Then, read a rhyme and have them beat their drums to the beat of the syllables.

> Psst...
> Find rhymes and songs in different languages for drumming to celebrate different cultures.

Mary Had A Little Lamb

Mary had a little lamb,

little lamb,
little lamb.
Mary had a little lamb,
Its fleece was white as snow.

Everywhere that Mary went,

Mary went,
Mary went.
Everywhere that Mary went,
The lamb was sure to go.

It followed her to school one day,

school one day,
school one day.
It followed her to school one day,
Which was against the rules.

It made the children laugh and play,

laugh and play,
laugh and play.
It made the children laugh and play,
To see a lamb at school.

Extension Ideas

✎ Look for more nursery rhymes on the internet or in your local library.

✎ Encourage children to write their own rhymes and songs to drum along with.

✎ Children may softly drum along with multi-cultural story books.

✎ Try turning drums over and drumming on the tin bottom for a different sound.

"Content Standards"

Reading

Phonemic Awareness

✎ Track auditorily each word in a sentence and each syllable in a word.

✎ Count the number of sounds in syllables and syllables in words.

Listening and Speaking

Comprehension

✎ Listen attentively.

Speaking Applications

✎ Recite poems, rhymes, songs, and stories.

Haiku Straw Painting

Staff Role and Space

Staff provide direction, supervision and encouragement.
Comfortable table and chairs.

Time Needed

Prep Time: Gathering of materials, especially the ink can take some time.
Minimum Time Needed:
Two 45-minute sessions (plus drying time)
    15 minutes to discuss and share Haiku poetry
    15-30 minutes to write poems
    15 minutes to straw paint with ink
    2 hours of drying time
    15 minutes to 'wash' with water colors

Supplies

White construction paper
Permanent markers
Straws
Black ink with dropper
Pencils
Water colors
Scrap paper

Adaptation/Modifications

✎ Remembering to enjoy the process, it may be necessary to allow children to experiment with their poetry. If it's not a true Haiku, it is ok.

Purpose

To provide opportunities for children to be creative through ink painting and poetry writing while learning about Haiku poetry.

Directions

1. Discuss Haiku poetry with the children. Post a few examples so children can refer to them often.

2. Drop a few tiny drops of black ink on each child's paper, making sure the ink is off to one side of the paper.

3. Have the children blow the ink around by using a straw. The children will discover that if they get the straw close to the paper, they can create long tree-like shapes. If they blow hard, they will create a splash.

4. Discuss with the children what their ink design might look like. Often, these designs of ink may inspire the poetry.

5. Let the ink dry. This may take a few hours.

6. With younger children, write a Haiku poem together. Older children can enjoy the experience of writing their own.

7. Have children write the poem on their white construction paper away from the ink.

8. After all the ink dries, have the children make a watercolor wash by using a paint brush and lightly covering the entire sheet of paper with water colors.

9. Mount dry paintings on a large black paper to create a border.

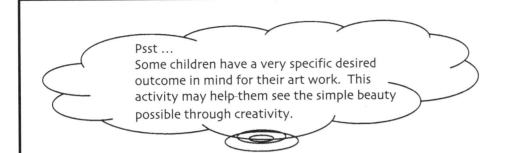

Psst ...
Some children have a very specific desired outcome in mind for their art work. This activity may help them see the simple beauty possible through creativity.

Characteristics of a Haiku Poem

✎ Has 3 lines and no more than 17 syllables is required. The traditional Japanese form further requires

Line 1: 5 syllables
Line 2: 7 syllables
Line 3: 5 syllables

✎ References nature

✎ Uses every day objects

✎ Can focus on any emotion

✎ Does not rhyme

Haiku Poetry Examples

Kójó
Night, and the moon!
My neighbor, playing on his flute -out of tune!

Basho
An old pond!
A frog jumps in-
The sound of water

Won't you come and see
loneliness? Just one leaf
from the kiri tree.

Extension Ideas

✎ Borrow Japanese Art books from the library to share with the children.
✎ Invite a Japanese parent or community member to share cultural activities with children.
✎ Discuss Japanese cooking and serve a simple Japanese snack.
✎ Add crumpled bits of tissue to the branches as blossoming flowers.
✎ Use a large sheet of butcher paper to create a group mural.
✎ Use a brown shopping bag for the paper and make the art work into a book cover.

"Content Standards"

Reading
Literary response and analysis
✎ Identify the use of rhythm, rhyme and alliteration in poetry.
Writing Strategies
Use descriptive words when writing
✎ Write descriptions that use concrete sensory details to present and support unified impressions of people, places, things and experiences.
Speaking Applications
✎ Recite short poems, rhymes and songs.

Hey, That's Me!

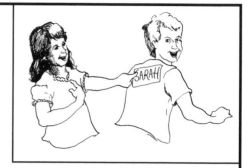

Staff Role and Space

Staff will give directions and supervise children.
Circle area, room to walk about.

Time

Prep Time: None
Minimum Time Needed:
45 minute session

Supplies

Sticky name tag badges, or pieces of scrap paper and tape.
Markers

Adaptation/Modifications

✎ The adult may stick a name tag on the back of each child to limit confusion with younger children.
✎ The adult may write the names in clear, large print for easier recognition.

Purpose

For children to learn to recognize their own written name and that of their friends.

Directions

1. Gather the children together to sit in a circle.

2. Pass out the name tags and have each child write their name on one tag. Do not put them on yet!

3. Collect the name tags and shuffle them up. Pass out one name tag per child. They can not have their own name, or that of the person next to them. They can not show anyone the name tag they have.

4. Now the children put the name tag they are holding onto the back of the person next to them. Remind them not to share the name they have.

5. When you say 'go', the children mingle about and try to find their own name on the back of another child

6. When they find their own name tag, they peel it off of the other person's back and put it on their own chest.

Psst...
You can repeat this activity over and over until the children can read their own names and the names of all the children in the program.

Psst ...
This is a fun activity to use with a new group of children. It's a great team builder!

Extension Ideas

✎ Challenge the children to write their first, middle and last names.

✎ Have children write other categories of words like colors they are wearing, favorite foods, favorite animals. Follow the same directions.

✎ Have the children write names of their favorite characters on the slips. Follow the directions as described. When the children find the character's name that they wrote, have them act out these characters.

"Content Standards"

Reading

Concepts about Print

✎ Understand that printed materials provide information.

Decoding and word recognition

✎ Read simple one-syllable and high-frequency words.

Writing

Penmanship

✎ Write uppercase and lowercase letters of the alphabet independently, attending to the form and proper spacing of the letters.

7. They continue to mingle until they have their own name tag and the name tag on their back is gone.

8. When finished, each child sits back down in circle.

9. When all children are seated, go around the circle and have children read their names.

How Are We Feeling?

Staff Role and Space

Supervision and direction while making the cards. Directions and encouragement during activity.

Drama area, or an open space such as a group circle area.

Time

Prep Time: 30 minutes to prepare index cards and select story
Minimum Time Needed:
45 minute session

Supplies

Index cards
Markers
Blackboard or chart paper
Drama props and clothing (optional)

Adaptation/Modifications

✎ Encourage children to create their own script.
✎ English as second language learners can use their home language while participating in activities.

Purpose

For children to read common words and express their feelings through drama.

Directions

Prepare Feeling Cards

1. You will need one Feeling Card, index card, per child participating.

2. Gather the children and have them brainstorm feelings. An older child or an adult can write the feelings on the board.

3. Have the children copy the different feelings onto the index cards. One feeling per card, and as many different feelings as possible. It is ok to have repeated feelings on cards.

4. Collect the cards from the children and shuffle the cards up.

Organize and enjoy the following activities using your cards.

Feelings to Suggest
(See the Feeling Words List on page 173 for other emotion words)

Happy	Tired
Sad	Excited
Angry	Disappointed
Lonely	Enthusiastic
Cheerful	Forlorn
Energetic	Lonely
Mad	Grouchy

Activity Ideas

Feelings Charades

1. Divide the children into even groups and divide the cards evenly between groups.

2. Taking turns, have the groups select players. The player chooses a card and acts out the feeling. The team guesses the feeling being acted out. The teams get a point for each feeling they guess correctly. Rotate players, giving each participant a chance to guess and also act.

The Same Story, a Different Feeling

1. Read the story *Mouse and the Lion* or *The Ant and the Grasshopper,* found on page 178, to the children. *(Check the website list in the back of the book for a link to over 100 Aesop's Fables)*

2. Assign roles and help children practice their roles.

3. Children will act out the role using different feelings. Let them choose which feeling they want to express while acting.

4. Try the same script using different feelings!

A Story of Feelings

1. Have your feeling cards face down on the table. Have each child pick a card and read it.

2. Begin telling a story. After one minute, the child sitting to your right begins adding onto the story. As the child tells their part of the story, they must include the feeling on the card they chose.

3. Continue the story around the circle. Each child gets one minute to add their feeling into the story.

4. Warning! The story gets very silly and everyone may not get to add their parts due to uncontrollable laughter.

Psst ...
Leave the cards out during free choice and the children will discover and invent new ways to use them.

5 to 8

"Content Standards"

Reading

Word Analysis, Fluency, and Systematic Vocabulary Development
✎ Match oral words to printed words.
✎ Identify letters and words.
Decoding and word recognition
✎ Read common, irregular sight words.
Comprehension and Analysis of Grade-Level-Appropriate Text
✎ Relate prior knowledge to textual information.

Suggested Readings with Children

✎ *Because of Winn-Dixie,* **Kate Dicamillo (For older children)**
✎ *I'm Gonna Like Me: Letting Off a Little Self-Esteem,* **Jamie Lee Curtis**

See the list of websites at the back of the book for the link to other stories that can be used for this activity.

Reproducibles on p. 173 & 178

Hug a Tree

Staff Role and Space

Staff should lead discussions, write down the vocabulary and provide support and supervision. They should also make sure that the children treat the tree with respect, i.e. not tearing the leaves or jabbing the bark with their pencils.

Need to go to a place with at least one tree, and inside where the children can write.

Time

Prep Time: Gathering of support books and materials.

Minimum Time Needed:
    Two 45-minute sessions

Supplies

Markers and crayons
Pencils or pens
Paper
Chart paper or blackboard
Books about trees
Children's Dictionary (Optional)
Children's Thesaurus (Optional)
Clip Boards (Optional)

Adaptation/Modifications

✎ Younger children will need more help writing the words on their pictures. Expect them to write fewer words and to draw more pictures.

✎ You can team children of different abilities together to do one picture.

✎   In groups with many English Language Learners, have them come up with the vocabulary in both languages.

Purpose

To increase vocabulary and write descriptive paragraphs.

Directions

1. Read a story related to trees. See the suggested resources for ideas. Have the children look through other books about trees.

2. Brainstorm different words about trees that they heard in the story and other words they might know related to trees.

3. Take a walk outside with the children and look at different trees. Have all the children choose one tree or let small groups choose their own tree.

4. Have the children really look at the tree. Have them talk about their impressions about:

> What it looks like. (You might want to see how many people it takes to encircle the tree trunk.)
>
> What the leaves are like.
>
> What it smells like. (Have them very carefully break off a little piece of bark and smell it. Teach them to be very respectful of all living things.)
>
> What it feels like.
>
> What living creatures are in or on the tree.
>
> How it makes them feel.
>
> What they would like to do with it.

5. Go back inside, and write down on a large writing surface, (a blackboard or chart paper) the following headings:

Looks Like	Smells Like	Feels Like	Living Creatures
	Makes me feel		Things to do with it

6. Have the children brainstorm different words that go under each heading, and write them down. (This is another good time to have them look at books about trees, so they can learn words that they can add to the list.)

7. Tell them to think of a name for their tree.

8. Have them draw their tree, write its name and write words or sentences on their drawing about the tree.

9. (Optional) Have them write a story, poem or report about their tree.

> Psst...
> If you want to learn more activities that relate to trees, check out PROJECT LEARNING TREE, an environmental education project sponsored by the Western Regional Environmental Education Council and the American Forest Foundation. This program provides free training and great material in every state. Go to their website at PLT.org.

Common Vocabulary Words Related to Trees

Things

Bark
Birds
Bough
Branches
Broad-Leafed
Buds
Cobwebs
Flower
Fruit
Leaves
Lichen
Limb
Moss
Nuts
Pine Cones
Pruned

Roots
Sap
Sapling
Seeds
Squirrels
Spiders
Stem
Tall
Trunk
Twigs
Wide
Vein

Sounds

Breezy
Chirping
Crunchy

Quiet
Rustling
Still

Texture/Smells

Aromatic
Coarse
Earthy
Even
Hardwood
Musty
Rough
Serrated
Sticky
Softwood
Sweet
Smooth
Woody

Suggested Resources

Fiction
✎ The Lorax, **Dr. Seuss**
✎ My Mother Talks to Trees, **Doris Gove**
✎ Old Elm Speak: Tree Poems, **Kate Kiesler**
✎ Tanya's Big Green Dream, **Linda Glaser**

Non-Fiction
✎ Bark (Would You Believe It), **Catherine Chambers**
✎ Be a Friend to a Tree, **Patricia Lauber**
✎ Forests for the Future (Protecting our Planet), **Edward Parker**
✎ I Wonder Why Trees Have Leaves: and Other Questions about Plants, **Andrew Charman**
✎ Once There Was a Tree, **Natalia Ramanova**
✎ Tell Me, Tree: All about Trees for Kids, **Gail Gibbons**
✎ Tree (Eyewitness Books), **David Burne**
✎ Trees, Leaves and Bark (Take Along Guide), **Diane Burns**
✎ The Tremendous Tree Book, **Barbara Brenner**

Extension Ideas

✎ Write a poem about a tree. Use the Concrete Poem format or a Name Poem format as described in those activities.
✎ Do Tree Rubbings and Bark Paintings.
✎ With a tree guide book, determine the names of the various trees in your area.
✎ See if you can locate streets on a city map that are named after trees.
✎ Visit a lumber yard or a sawmill if there is one in your community.
✎ Have a forester come and talk to your participants. Check with the State or Federal Forest Services for speakers.
✎ Plant a tree or trees in your area. See the story, Tanya's Big Green Dream for inspiration. Take care of it over the year. Keep a journal and record how it changes. If there is only a little space, plant the tree in a large container. You can then decorate it for the different holidays.

"Content Standards"

Reading
Vocabulary and Concept Development
✎ Identify and sort common words in basic categories.

Writing
✎ Writing brief narratives describing an experience.
✎ Group related ideas and maintain a consistent focus.
✎ Write descriptions.

Human Letters & Words

Staff Role and Space

Staff will call out the letters and support and supervise.
Floor or outside area clean enough for children to lay down. The amount of running in the *Word Relay* will depend on the size of the area.

Time

Prep Time: Time to make the letter sets for Activity Three—30 minutes

Minimum Time Needed:
    Could be a very quick activity or up to 45 minutes.

Supplies

Slips of paper
Construction paper for the letters
Container
Mats to lay on (optional)

Adaptation/Modifications

✎ If you work with English Learners, you can use the letters or the symbols of their primary language.
✎ Make sure that children who are physically challenged are also included in the letter making and the races. The children will find a way to include them if as an adult you just include them naturally.

Purpose

To reinforce letter and sound recognition.

Directions

Body Language: Letters

1. Divide the children into groups of five. (This is how many children are needed to form most letters.)

2. Put a different letter of the alphabet on each slip of paper and put the slips in a box or container.

3. Have the children pick one slip of paper and have them say the name of the letter.

4. Have them figure out how they are going to make the letter with their bodies.

5. Have them stand or lie on the floor forming the letter. Let the other children guess what letter they are making.

6. Have children form common blends or diagraphs. (See the list of blends and digraphs on page 174.)

Body Language: Words (For groups of at least 15 participants)

1. Write three-letter words that have short vowel sounds on slips of paper. If you have at least 20 participants, you can write four letter words that have blends.

2. Pull out one slip and have the participants decide how they are going to form the word with their bodies.

Psst...
Different children have different learning styles. Most activities in schools involve activities stressing the visual or auditory. But for those children who learn best through movement (kinesthetics), this activity is great for helping them learn their alphabet and letter sounds.

Word Relay (Can be done with as few as three children)

1. Write each alphabet letter, individually on construction paper to make a set of 26 letters. You should make enough sets so that each group can grab two of the same letters if needed to spell the word. (*You can have the children make these.*)

2. Put the letters in a pile. If you want to have more movement in this activity, put the piles of letters on one end of the room, and the children on the other end.

3. Group participants in threes.

4. Call out a word. Have the children run to the letter piles and find the letters that spells the word.

5. Have the children go back to a designated space, with each child holding one card in front of them and standing in the right order to spell out the word.

6. You can make this a competitive game between teams, giving points to the group that forms the words the fastest.

Sample Words

hat fat mat bad cap jam pack glad pan

bed fell ten chest pet west met cell red

kick did rig mill brick slid pin wing drip

dock top pot chop knot grub shop spot

tub luck rug drum sun strut duck sun jut

bail chain bake blame bank gate name snail

beat weep sleet twice bride lime five

boat gold stole phone rose

by cry sly try

Extension Ideas

✎ Do activity three with the children's spelling words. You will need to have sets that include at least five sets of each letter if the words are longer.

✎ If you do the exercise outside, have the children use sidewalk chalk to outline the "living letters." When the children get up, they can see what they formed.

✎ Have the children run "word" relay races:

1. The first child of the team runs and gets the letters to spell a word given by the adult.
2. The child runs back and the team forms the word as described in activity three.
3. Then the next child in the team runs.
4. Repeat until the last member gets back.
5. First team to finish, wins.

"Content Standards"
Reading
Word Analysis

✎ Recognize and name all uppercase and lowercase letters of the alphabet.

✎ Blend vowel-consonant sounds orally to make words or syllables.

✎ Match all consonant and short-vowel sounds to appropriate letters.

✎ Read simple one-syllable words.

✎ Generate the sounds from all letters and letter patterns and blend those sounds into recognizable words.

✎ Recognize and use knowledge of spelling patterns.

✎ Use knowledge of complex word families to decode unfamiliar words.

Reproducible on p. 174

It's All About Me!

Staff Role and Space

Staff will explain process, supervise and assist children.
A comfortable writing area and arts and craft area.

Time

Prep Time:
Time to gather materials.
Minimum time needed:
45 minute session

Supplies

Lined paper
Pencils
Optional:
Construction paper
Markers, crayons
Paints
Old magazines
Scissors
Glue, paste
Clothes hangers
Cameras or pictures of the children
String or yarn
Paper punch

Adaptation/Modifications

✎ For children not yet writing, encourage them to draw pictures and have them dictate captions to an experienced writer.
✎ For children that speak English as a second language, encourage them to write in their native language.

Purpose

To have children write descriptions of themselves and display them in creative ways.

Directions

1. Gather the children around and explain to them that they will be describing themselves. They may include everything and anything about themselves that they would like to share with others. Explain to them that writings about one's self are called autobiographies.

2. On the chalkboard, brainstorm descriptive words they may want to include in their autobiographies. Leave these up so they may use them.

3. Encourage the children to enjoy the process of describing themselves. Have them write a few words about themselves. The following topics may help:

> ✎ Physical description
> ✎ Favorite things to do
> ✎ My family

After the children have their description written, complete one of the following display activities.

Psst ...
All of these activities make wonderful gifts for parents or other loved ones.

Ways to Display Autobiographies

1. Hanger Mobiles

a. Children will write items from their autobiographical list on shapes cut out from construction paper (clouds, circles, cars, animals, etc.).

b. Paper punch holes at top of shapes and tie one piece of string or yarn per shape. Each shape should have a different length of string.

c. Tie the shapes to the hanger and adjust to have them hang without tangling. Hang up and enjoy!

2. Hand Prints

a. Supervise children directly as they make their hand prints on a large sheet of construction paper using brightly colored paints.

b. When dry, have children write their autobiographical information around their hand prints.

3. Self Portraits

a. Have children draw or paint a self-portrait.

b. When portraits are dry, have children add their autobiographical information to their portraits.

4. Silhouettes

a. Using a bright light (an overhead projector works well), cast the child's profile shadow on a black piece of construction paper taped to the wall.

b. Trace the shadow image onto the black paper and cut out. Next, glue this portrait 'shadow' onto a large sheet of white construction paper.

c. The child now copies their autobiographical information on the white paper, around their shadow.

Chloe's Sample

Black Curly Hair
Brown Eyes
Soccer and Riding my Bike
Mommy, Daddy and Grandpa

Extension Ideas

✎ Create an "It's All about Us" group bulletin board. Individuals and groups, Scouts, Teams, etc., can be represented here.

✎ Create a video with children narrating their autobiographies.

✎ Use snippets of the autobiographies for a yearbook or photo album.

"Content Standards"

Reading

Structural Features of Literature

✎ Distinguish common forms of literature.

Writing

Organization and Focus

✎ Use letters and phonetically spelled words to write about experiences, stories, people, objects, or events.

✎ Group related ideas and maintain a consistent focus.

Spelling

✎ Spell independently by using prephonetic knowledge, sounds of the alphabet, and knowledge of letter names.

Label That Thing

Staff Role and Space

The staff members must start the activity and then supervise and support.
Can be done in any space.

Time

Prep Time: Time to write the words or phrases on the post'em notes. - 15 minutes
Minimum Time Needed:
10 to 45 minutes

Supplies

Post'em notes or slips of paper and scotch tape
Markers
Children's Dictionary (optional)
(If you want to get really fancy with words, you might need an adult dictionary.)

Adaptation/Modifications

✎ You can put easy or hard words on the labels. You should probably have dictionaries available for the hard words.
(Example: You can use "friend" for young readers and "confidant" for older participants.)
✎ Partner better readers with readers having difficulty. Make sure the slower readers are in charge of holding the labels.
✎ The area that you use can vary from a classroom to the whole building and even outdoors.

Purpose

To have the children practice sight word recognition.

Directions

1. Write names of objects found in the after-school program site on post'em notes.

2. Pair up the children.

3. Give them the slips and have them post them around the room.

Other things you can do

a. Make it a race. You will have to make a set for each team.

b. Give them slips with just letters on them and have them find objects that begin with the letters.

c. Write the words in a phrase like "on the desk," "under the clock," "beside the door."

d. If you are working with bilingual children, write the words in their language and in English.

Psst...
Many children have trouble with understanding the meaning of prepositions. This is a great activity to help them learn them if you write the words in a phrase.

Psst....
If you are outside, your words will be related to objects found outside: "tree," "grass," "asphalt."

Examples of Label Words

Easy	Harder
Door	Opening
Window	Casement
Clock	Chronometer
Desk	Escritoire
Chair	Gluteus Support
Shelf	Storage Unit
Wall	Partition
Closet	Cupboard
Green Board	Writing Plank
Water Fountain	H_2O Dispenser
Chalk	Pulverized Limestone writing instrument
Crayons	Wax Writing instruments
Pencil	Writing Utensil
Book	Tome
Sign	Signage
Game	Entertainment
Calendar	Date Organizer
Friend	Confidant

Extension Ideas

✎ Scavenger hunts are a lot of fun. Prepare a similar list, but include only those objects that children can bring back.

✎ Have children make a book, putting a picture or a drawing of the object and its name on each page. See "My Own Letter Book" for an idea on how to make a book.

✎ Make a treasure map or have the children make a treasure map that gives directions to the different objects that they need to label.

✎ Read alphabet picture books to the children. Talk about the pictures and the labels in the books. Have older children make alphabet books for younger children. See "My Own Letter Book" activity for examples of good alphabet books.

"Content Standards"

Reading

Decoding

✎ Recognize and name all uppercase and lowercase letters of the alphabet.

✎ Read common irregular sight words.

Vocabulary Development

✎ Classify grade-appropriate categories of words.

Paper Plate Puppet Show

Staff Role and Space

Staff should read the story, give initial directions and provide support and supervision.

Can be done in any space, but best if participants can work at tables.

Time

Prep Time: Time to gather all the materials necessary.

Minimum Time Needed:

At least three 45 minute sessions:
  Session 1 to read and discuss the story
  Session 2 to make puppets
  Session 3 to write the play and perform

Supplies

Dinner size paper plates
Crayons and markers
Construction paper
Jumbo Craft Sticks - 6 " by 3/4"
Yarn
Scissors
Glue
"Wiggle Eyes" assortments (optional)
Fabric (optional)

Adaptation/Modifications

✎ Older children can select their own stories and read them on their own. They will then need to give a summary of the story before they put on their show.

✎ English learners can perform their plays in their home language.

Purpose

To be able to identify elements of character, and to retell a story.

Directions

1. Read a story to the children. See the Resources section in the back of the book for suggested stories.

2. Have children name the different characters in the story and what the characters look like, act like and what they do.

3. Have each child make a paper plate puppet that represents one of the characters.

4. Form pairs of children who have selected different characters.

5. Have them come up with a short puppet show based on a scene in the story using their paper plate puppets.

6. Have the children perform their skits.

Example:
Story: *Jamaica Louise James* by Amy Hest
Characters:
      Jamaica   Her grandmother
      Her mother   People in the subway
Events:
   Jamaica talking with her grandmother about her job

   Grandmother's reaction to the painting in the subway

   Two of the people in the subway talking about their picture

   Jamaica Louise talking to her mother about her birthday idea

Making Paper Plate Puppets

1. Take a dinner-size paper plate and place it with the edges facing outward. (Fig. 1)

2. Draw eyes, nose and mouth or glue pieces of construction paper cut out in the shape of eyes, nose and mouth onto the paper plate.

3. Draw the shapes of ears onto construction paper. (These shapes can be as simple as triangles or semi-circles.) Glue the ears onto the sides of the paper plate.

4. Glue the craft stick onto the back of the plate with the end extending below the plate so that it can be used as a handle. (Fig. 2)

5. Glue yarn on the top and over the back of the plate to make hair. (Fig. 3)

6. If you want to, use fabric to make "clothes" for the puppet by gluing onto the front of the craft stick.

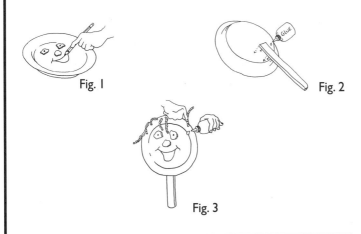

Fig. 1

Fig. 2

Fig. 3

Suggested Resources for Puppets

The Muppets Make Puppets! Book and Puppet Kit: How to Make Puppets out of All Kinds of Stuff Around Your House, Cheryl Henson

Check the suggested websites at the back of the book for more resources in puppet making.

Extension Ideas
✎ Have the children write their own plays based on characters that they create.
✎ Perform the plays and skits for other groups and parents. Have the children make a stage for their puppets.
✎ Plan and carry out a puppet theme, making different kinds of puppets over a period of time. See the websites listed on this page for lots more ways to make puppets.
✎ Invite a puppeteer to come and talk to the participants.
✎ Watch one of the Muppet Movies and talk about the way they used puppets.

"Content Standards"
Reading
Comprehension and Analysis of Text
✎ Retell familiar stories.

Narrative Analysis
✎ Identify and describe the elements of characters, settings, and important events.
✎ Determine what characters are like by what they say and do and by how the author or illustrator portrays them.

Speaking
Speaking Applications
✎ Describe people, places, things.
✎ Recount experiences or present stories.

My Own Letter Book

Staff Role and Space

Staff should give initial directions and provide support and supervision.
Can be done in any space, but best if participants can work at tables.

Time

Prep Time: Time to gather materials.
Minimum Time Needed:
At least two 45 minutes sessions, but could take longer. You might have children work on one letter a week.

Supplies

Markers and crayons
14 sheets of construction paper
Yarn
Three-hole punch
Old magazines, catalogs, old calendars
Scissors
Glue
Alphabet books
Letter Stencils (optional)

Adaptation/Modifications

✎ Two or three children can work on the same book, each taking different letters.
✎ For older children, they can put the letter of their name on each page, and find things that they like that start with the letter.

Purpose

To reinforce the names and sounds of letters.

Directions

1. Read an alphabet book to the children. Talk about how the illustrations are all about the letter.

2. Punch holes using a three-hole punch along the margin of 14 sheets of construction paper.

3. Tie the sheets together with yarn.

4. Start the project by having the children make covers.

✎ Have the children put a title for their book on the cover. For example: "Carrie's Alphabet Book."

✎ Have them write Author: and then their name, and Illustrator: and then their name.

✎ Then have them decorate the cover.

5. Have the children write or stencil one big and small letter of the alphabet on each page, until each page is labeled with a letter.

6. Go through magazines and catalogs to find pictures of things that start with different letters. Cut them out and glue them on the right page. The children can also draw pictures of objects that start with the letter.

7. Help the children label the pictures.

Psst...
In English, many words start with letters that are spelled one way, but sound differently. For instance, phone starts with "ph" but sounds like it starts with /f/. You will have to make a decision on how to talk to children about whether the pictures they choose have to start with the same letter as the sound or teach that different letters sometimes can make different sounds.

Alphabet Book Themes

You can ask children to make alphabet books that are about one subject. Here are some ideas:

Animals	School
Names	Food
Transportation	Colors
Favorite Activities	

Suggested Alphabet Books

✎ *A, My Name is Alice,* **J. Bayer**

✎ *Ashanti to Zulu: African Traditions,* **M. Musgrove**

✎ *C is for Curious: An ABC of Feelings,* **W. Hubbard**

✎ *The Dinosaur Alphabet Book,* **J. Pallotta**

✎ *Eating the Alphabet: Fruits and Vegetables from A to Z,* **L. Ehlert**

✎ *The Icky Bug Alphabet Book,* **J. Pallotta**

✎ *Jambo Means Hello: Swahili Alphabet Book,* **M. Feelings**

✎ *The Monster Book of ABC Sounds,* **A. Snow**

✎ *The Letters are Lost,* **Lisa Campbell Ernst**

✎ *Tomorrow's Alphabet,* **G. Shannon**

✎ *26 Letters and 99 Cents,* **T. Hoban**

Extension Ideas

✎ Have older children read their books to younger children or donate their books to hospital children's wards.

✎ Have the children play the game "Label that Thing" before doing this activity.

✎ Make this activity part of a Book Making theme that includes other styles of book making. There are examples of hinged books and other types of books in other sections.

✎ Have a book binder come and talk to your group or go visit a shop or company that binds their reports. Many big businesses have in-house printing departments.

"Content Standards"

Reading

Concept About Print

✎ Match oral words to printed words.

✎ Identify the title, author and illustrator of a book.

Decoding and Word Recognition

✎ Match all consonant and short-vowel sounds to appropriate words.

Vocabulary and Concept Development

✎ Identify and sort common words in basic categories.

Phonemic Awareness

✎ Distinguish initial sounds in words.

✎ Older children can make theme books: animals, transportation, music.

✎ Older children can also make alphabet books to give younger children.

✎ If you work with bilingual children, use words from both languages.

Name Poems: Acrostics

Staff Role and Space

Staff should give initial directions and provide support and supervision.
Can be done in any space, but best if participants can work at tables.

Time

Prep Time: Time to gather materials.
Minimum Time Needed:
   At least one 45-minute session

Supplies

Black marker
Markers and crayons
Construction paper
Chart paper/blackboard
Children's Thesaurus (optional)
Children's Dictionary (optional)
Letter stencils (optional)

Adaptation/Modifications

✏ If you work with bilingual children, they can write the poem in their home language.

✏ For children, who can not read or write yet, they can dictate their ideas to an adult.

✏ Children who can not read or write yet can write their name, and then decorate the paper with pictures that start with the letters of their name.

Purpose

To write descriptive sentences and increase vocabulary.

Directions

1. Have the children brainstorm the following:
   ✏ Their favorite things
   ✏ What they look like
   ✏ Where they live
   ✏ What they like to do
   ✏ Their personalities

2. Write their ideas down on chart paper or on a board so they can refer to them later.

3. Write their names down vertically on one side of the paper with black markers.

4. With the ideas that the children came up with during the brainstorming, have them find words that match the letters in the name and write them beside the matching letter. For example, words like "caring" or "cat-lover" would go by the letter **C**.

5. If they do not have any words to match the letter, have them look in a children's dictionary or thesaurus for ideas. Make sure the words they select match their likes and dislikes, looks, personalities.

6. After they have written their poems, have them decorate the paper with pictures and designs that further illustrate who they are.

Psst...
Name poems are examples of Acrostic poems. You can use the same process with any theme. For instance, if you are doing art projects, you can have the children write down vertically the letters of the colors they used and write a poem describing their object.

Resource
Check out **ProTeacher Page: What's in a Name?** for more great ideas of other activities using the children's names. **The address is found on the website list in the back of the book.**

Extension Ideas

✎ Have the children find out the history of their name by asking their parents why they gave them their name. Have them share this information with the other participants.

✎ Make a *Participant Name Book* by stapling all the participants' poems together. Make a cover sheet that the group can decorate. Include the book in the after-school library.

✎ Have each child make a poetry book, including Name poems, Concrete poems and Autobiographical poems found in this book.

✎ Read the book, *Chrysanthemum* by **Kevin Henkes** and talk about whether the children like their names and how to handle teasing about their names.

"Content Standards"

Reading
Vocabulary
✎ Describe common objects and events in both general and specific language.

Literary Response and Analysis
✎ Distinguish common forms of literature.

Writing
✎ Write descriptions that use concrete sensory details to present and support unified impressions of people, places, things and experiences.

Speaking Applications
✎ Provide descriptions with careful attention to sensory detail.
✎ Recite poems, rhymes, songs and stories.

Playing with Song Lyrics
Three Little Monkeys

Staff Role and Space

Staff will lead the initial activities and then support and supervise.
The children should be able to easily see the chart paper and have table space to work on their drawings.

Time

Prep Time: 15 minutes to write lyrics on chart paper, and cut up song lyric sheets.
Minimum Time Needed:
   45-minute session

Supplies

Song lyrics
White construction paper
Crayons/Markers
Pre-cut lyric strips
Chart paper or blackboard

Adaptation/Modifications

✎ Teach songs in different languages, especially if you have children whose home language is not English.
✎ For older children, especially middle-school children, you can find lyrics for popular songs and follow the same exercise. Care will need to be taken in the selection. They might want to use designs rather than draw pictures to illustrate the lyrics.

Purpose

To increase reading fluency.

Directions

1. Before the children arrive:
   ✎ Clearly write the song lyrics of *Three Little Monkeys* on chart paper or a board.
   ✎ Cut up the song lyric strips so that each child has a set, or there is a set for a small group. Song lyric strips can be found on page 179.

2. Sing the song together with the children, pointing to the words on the chart while you sing. Have them repeat the song a few times until you are sure they are familiar with the lyrics.

3. Have the children take turns identifying words on the chart. For instance, ask a child to point out the word "monkey" on the chart.

4. (Optional) Have the children identify words that begin with a certain letter. For instance, all the words that begin with an /M/ or /m/, or words that have short vowel sounds like short /e/ in "bed," "fell."

5. Hand out the song lyric strips. Have the children put them in order and glue them to a piece of construction paper.

6. Have children decorate the paper, drawing pictures that illustrate the song.

7. Sing the song again before leaving.

Psst....
If you have trouble carrying a tune, find tapes or CD's of the song. Also remember young children don't care how you sound. Just be enthusiastic!

Three Little Monkeys

(*No actual melody, accent on the underlined words*)

Three little mon<u>keys</u> jumping on the <u>bed</u>
One fell <u>off</u> and bumped his <u>head</u>
So Momma <u>called</u> the doctor <u>and</u> the doctor <u>said</u>
No more mon<u>keys</u> jumping on the <u>bed</u>!

Two little mon<u>keys</u> jumping on the <u>bed</u>
One fell <u>off</u> and bumped his <u>head</u>
So Momma <u>called</u> the doctor <u>and</u> the doctor <u>said</u>
No more mon<u>keys</u> jumping on the <u>bed</u>!

One little mon<u>key</u> jumping on the <u>bed</u>
He fell <u>off</u> and bumped his <u>head</u>
So Momma <u>called</u> the doctor <u>and</u> the doctor <u>said</u>
No more mon<u>keys</u> jumping on the <u>bed</u>!

No little mon<u>keys</u> jumping on the <u>bed</u>
None fell <u>off</u> and bumped his <u>head</u>
So Momma <u>called</u> the doctor and the doctor <u>said</u>
Put those monkeys back in <u>bed</u>!

Resources

Websites for Lyrics
See the Website list at the back of the book for great links for other songs that could be used.

- *De Colores & Other Latin American Folk Songs for Children*, **Jose-Luis Orozco**
- *KidsSong* Series, **Nancy and John Cassidy**
- *Kids Make Music! Clapping and Tapping From Bach to Rock!* **Avery Hart**
- *Sing Through the Day: Eighty Songs for Children*, **Maryls Swinger** (Comes with a CD; emphasizes multicultural selections; the reading level is upper elementary)
- *Step It Down: Games, Plays, Songs and Stories from the Afro-American Heritage*, **Bessie Jones**

Extension Ideas
- You can do this activity with a different song once a week and have the children make a song book. With a three hole punch, make holes and use circle clips to hold the pages together.
- Put on a music performance for parents and other participants.
- There are many picture books based on popular songs. See the list below for suggestions. Read the book to the children after you have taught them the song.
- Invite people in the community to come in and teach the children their favorite songs.

"Content Standards"
Reading
Concept About Print
- Match oral words to printed words.
Decoding and Word Recognition
- Match all consonant and short vowel sounds to appropriate words.
Vocabulary and Concept Development
- Identify and sort common words in basic categories.

Illustrated Books Based on Popular Children's Songs

- *The Eensy-Weensy Spider*, **Mary Ann Haberman**
- *Follow the Drinking Gourd*, **Jeanette Winter** (Great book for Black History Month)
- *Hush!: A Thai Lullaby*, **Minfong Ho**
- *Oh, A Hunting We will Go*, **John Langstaff**
- *There was an Old Lady who Swallowed a Fly*, **Timms Taback.**
- *The Wheels on the Bus*, **Raffi**

Reproducible on p. 179

Sponge Garden

Staff Role and Space
*Provide direction, supervision and encouragement to continue observation and journaling **over time**.*
A comfortable place to sit and write.

Time
Prep Time: Time to gather materials
Minimum Time Needed:
   45-minute session to plant gardens, make journal and write initial observations
   Ongoing journal entry opportunities

Supplies
Plastic or aluminum containers large enough to hold a sponge
Sponges with large pores
2 different types of seeds, one large and one small
Water
Pens, pencils and markers
For making the journal
      Popsicle sticks
      Hole punch
      Rubber bands
      Markers/crayons for decorating

Adaptation/Modifications
✎ As a group, discuss the development of the seeds. Then, the adult may write sample sentences on a board for children to copy into their journals.
✎ Older children will want to include more information in their journals.
✎ Instead of individual gardens, create a large group sponge garden.

Purpose
To have children explore gardening and journal keeping to encourage writing organization and concept development.

Directions
1. Open discussion with children about whether large seeds produce large plants and small seeds produce small plants. Group brainstorm and record highlights of the discussion.

2. Explain to children that they will be planting small and large seeds in a sponge, creating a sponge garden.

3. Have children draw a line on top of the sponge, dividing it in half.

4. Give the children the large seeds and have them poke them down into the sponge on one side of the line. Use approximately 5-8 large seeds. Mark this side of the sponge with a Popsicle stick that has the name of the plant written on it.

5. Next, provide the children with twice as many small seeds and have them poke them into the other top half of the sponge. Add the Popsicle markers to this side.

6. Pour approximately one inch of water into the containers. Set the sponge into the container. The sponge will soak up some of the water. Continue to add water as necessary to keep half of the sponge immersed.

7. Sponge gardens should be set near a window so they can enjoy natural light each day. **Sponges need to be moist at all times. Make sure the children water them daily.**

> Psst ...
> Huge seeds, such as sunflower seeds, are fun to watch and they grow quickly!

8. Have children make a popsicle journal. Directions are below.

9. Storing the journals and writing supplies near the gardens promotes and encourages regular entries. Children benefit from having a set time daily or weekly to write in their journals. They will enjoy observing their gardens to determine whether or not the large seeds produce larger plants and how fast the seeds grow.

10. When plants stop growing, or need to be re-planted in a garden, complete the project with a group discussion of whether or not large seeds produce large plants!

Popsicle Stick Journal

1. On half sheets of paper, punch two holes on top of a stack of paper (15 sheets). The holes should be measured approximately 1 inch from top edge of paper and 1.5 inches apart from another. (Fig. 1)

2. Feed a rubber band through the two holes from the bottom of paper. (Fig. 2)

3. Slide a popsicle stick through the two hoops of the rubber band on top of the paper. If this is too loose, use a smaller rubber band or add more paper. (Fig. 3)

4. Slipping a pencil in on top of the popsicle stick keeps the pencil handy!

Extension Ideas

✎ Modify the "Bug Map" found in the *Creature Feature* activity to use with this activity.

✎ Visit a nursery in your community for a field trip.

✎ Plan a garden at your site. Often container gardens work well at school sites. Ask parents and community members to contribute different size pots.

✎ Check out gardening books at the library for the children.

✎ Experiment to see what else you can grow seeds in!

✎ Have children create colorful covers for their Sponge Garden Journals. Post their entries for others to enjoy.

"Content Standards"
Reading
Vocabulary and Concept Development
✎ Classify grade appropriate categories of words.
Writing Strategies
Organization and focus
✎ Select a focus when writing.
✎ Use descriptive words when writing.

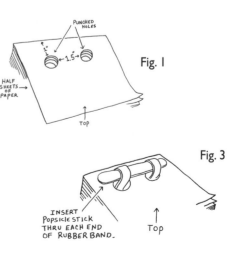

Fig. 1

PUNCHED HOLES

1.5"

HALF SHEETS OF PAPER

TOP

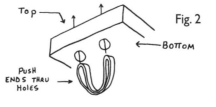

Top

BOTTOM

PUSH ENDS THRU HOLES

Fig. 2

Fig. 3

INSERT POPSICLE STICK THRU EACH END OF RUBBER BAND.

Top

5 to 8

Story Board

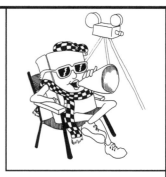

Staff Role and Space

The adult will read the story, lead the discussion and support and supervise the activity.

Can be done in any space, but best if participants can quietly listen to a story, and spread out into small groups.

Time

Prep Time: Gathering of materials
Minimum Time Needed:

Two 45-minute sessions:

Session 1 to read the book and decide on events

Session 2 to review the book and draw the events

Supplies

Picture Books/Early Readers
White 8" x 15" construction paper
Markers or crayons

Adaptation/Modifications

✎ The story can be read orally by an adult or small groups of children can read together.

✎ The events that are going to be drawn can be chosen by:

the whole group
the staff member
the children in the group

Purpose

To have participants practice story sequencing skills.

Directions

1. The children listen or read a story that includes a series of events.

2. Either as a large group, in small groups or individually the children decide on the major events. Make sure they include what happened first and how the story ended.

3. Have each child fold a piece of construction paper into 8ths by folding the paper in half, and then in half again, and then in half again.

4. Have the children number each of the boxes made by the folds.

5. Draw a separate picture for each of the major events, putting the pictures in order as they happened in the story.

6. Have the children retell the story using their pictures.

When done in small groups:

1. Have the children each decide which event they are going to draw.

2. Each child in the group draws one picture of an event on a full piece of paper.

3. Have the children line up with their pictures in order of when the events happened in the story.

4. Have each child tell their part of the story based on their picture.

Psst...
Have the children take their storyboard home
and tell the story to their parents using the
pictures as cues for remembering the story.
This is a great way to have the children
communicate with their parents.

Creating the Story Board

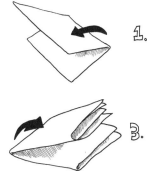

Suggested Books

Most of these books are also available in Spanish.

- ✎ *The Birthday Swap,* **Loretta Lopez**
- ✎ *A Chair for my Mother,* **Vera Williams**

(This is a tricky one because there is a flashback in the story.)

- ✎ *Ruby the Copycat,* **Peggy Rathmann**
- ✎ *The Relatives Came,* **Cynthia Rylant**
- ✎ *Jamaica's Find,* **Juanita Havill**
- ✎ *The Meanest Thing to Say,* **Bill Cosby**
- ✎ *The Outside Dog,* **Charlotte Pomerantz**

Extension Ideas

✎ Have the participants complete the "Making a Movie" worksheet found on page 180 for a story they have read.

✎ Make up a play using the story board to plan the scenes. Video tape the play.

✎ Invite a film maker to talk about the use of storyboarding in making movies.

✎ Many expanded DVD's of popular Disney movies have in their extra material, examples of storyboards. Show the children the section on the storyboarding before they watch the movie.

"Content Standards"

Reading

Literacy Response and Analysis

✎ Retell familiar stories.

✎ Identify and describe the elements of plot, setting and character's in a story, as well as the story's beginning, middle and ending.

✎ Recalling details.

Reproducible on p. 180

Throwing for a Word

Staff Role and Space

Staff should give initial directions and provide support and supervision.
Enough floor or ground space to set up the cups.

Time

Prep Time: 15 minutes to get the cups taped and slips inside.
Minimum Time Needed:
As little as 20 minutes and up to 45 minutes.

Supplies

Plastic or Styrofoam cups
Masking tape
Small objects to toss (buttons, pebbles, chips)
Slips of paper
Paper to record responses

Adaptations/Modifications

✎ Have children who are more advanced in their skills be the recorders.
✎ Change the throwing distance depending on the motor skills of the children, and any challenges based on physical impairments.
✎ Older children can be the coaches for younger children.
✎ You can put prefixes or suffixes on the slips of paper for older children. (See appendix for a list of prefixes and suffixes.)

Purpose

To match all consonant and short-vowel sounds to appropriate letters and to read common word families.

Directions

1. Using masking tape, tape the bottoms of at least 10 cups in a straight line to the floor. Make sure the cup rims are close together with no space in between.

2. Put slips of paper on the inside bottom of the cups with either individual letters, or consonant blends and digraphs, or letter families (like –at, -op, -ed). See pages 174 & 176 for blends and digraphs and suggested word family endings.

3. Assign a recorder or children can take turns. Their job is to keep track of the words that the children say.

4. Have the children take turns tossing a small object one at a time into the cups. They must say a word that either begins or ends with the letters, or make a word with the word family depending on what is written on the slip.

5. Have them keep score of the words that they compose.

Fun Literacy Activities for After-School Programs

> Psst…
> The role of after-school programs is to support learning, not to directly instruct, unless that is part of the actual mission of your after-school program. Keep the emphasis on fun in these kinds of literacy activities.

Variations

✎ Put sight vocabulary or spelling words in the cups. Have someone other than the one who tossed the object read the word in the cup. The child has to spell the word correctly in order to get the point.

✎ Break the children into groups. The team members think of as many words as they can using the letters or word families. The team with the most words wins.

✎ Once an object lands in a cup, no one else can use that cup. The game ends when all the cups have an object in them. If an object lands in a cup that already has another one, the child can not earn a point.

Resources for Other Games with Letters and Word Families

✎ *Words their Way: Word Study for Phonic, Vocabulary, and Spelling Instruction*, **Donald Bear, Marcia Invernizzi, Shane Templeton, Francine Johnston**

✎ *Phonics from A to Z*, **Wiley Blevins**

✎ *Quick-and Easy Learning Games: Phonics*, **Wiley Blevins**

✎ *Phonics Games Kids Can't Resist*, **Michelle Ramsey**

Extension Ideas

✎ Have an "academic" carnival with different booths that have games that reinforce reading and math. Have each of your groups in the program, sponsor and manage a booth.

✎ You could do the same activity to reinforce math skills by putting math problems in the bottom of the cups.

✎ Give the children some materials like cups, paper, sticks, small objects, cans, etc and have them invent a game that they will teach to other children. They will write their game rules for other children to read.

"Content Standards"
Reading
Decoding and Word Recognition
✎ Match all consonant and short-vowel sounds to appropriate words.
✎ Read common irregular sight words.
Phonemic Awareness
✎ Distinguish initial sounds in words.

Reproducibles on p. 174 & 176

Tongue Twisters

Staff Role and Space

Staff should give initial directions and provide support and supervision.
Can be done in any space, but if you want to do art projects with the activities it is best if participants can work at tables.

Time

Prep Time: Writing the tongue twisters on slips of paper should take about 15 minutes.

Minimum Time Needed:
    At least one 45-minute session.

Supplies

Copies of the tongue twisters
Paper
Markers/crayons/pencils
Children's dictionaries

Adaptation/Modifications

✎ Two or three children can work on practicing tongue twisters together.
✎ Older children can work with longer and more sophisticated tongue twisters. See the suggested resources for longer tongue twisters.
✎ For younger children, the staff member could work with the whole group to come up with tongue twisters.
✎ Find tongue twisters in the home language of your bilingual students.
✎ You can have fun with tongue twisters anytime. When you need to fill just a few minutes, use a tongue twister.
✎ For older children, show how adding concrete verbs and extra adjectives make tongue twisters even more fun.

Purpose

To reinforce phonemic awareness of initial sounds, and to practice public speaking and to use descriptive words when writing.

Directions

1. Explain that tongue twisters are phrases that are hard to pronounce, especially when you say them fast.

2. Do warm-ups. Have the children repeat a few tongue twisters together. Repeat the short ones at least 10 times to get the full effect.

Tongue Twister Game:
1. Break your group into two teams. Pair two people together, one from each team.

2. Give each child a tongue twister on a slip of paper. Have them take turns repeating the tongue twister three times quickly. If they pronounce the phrase correctly each time, they get two points for their team.

3. The staff member or older children should keep track of the points.

4. The team that gets the most points, wins.

Writing Tongue Twisters
1. Put children into groups of three or four.
2. Have them each answer the following questions using words that start with the same letter as the first letter in each of their names.

    ✎ What did s/he do?

    ✎ Where?

    ✎ When?

    ✎ How?

For example, a child whose name is Cathy might come up with: **Cathy**
What did she do? *Cleaned closets, crept, closed crates.*
Where? *In craters, near Cathay*
When? *At Christmas, after crashing, during church*
How? *Carefully, crisply, courageously*

3. Have each child write a tongue twister using the phrases that the team came up with using their name. You do not have to use every category.

Example: **Cathy carefully cleaned closets near Cathay at Christmas.**

4. Have the children illustrate their tongue twister.

5. Have the children challenge each other using their own tongue twisters.

Sample Tongue Twisters

(reproducible on page 181)

1. Peter Piper picked a peck of pickled peppers.
Did Peter Piper pick a peck of pickled peppers?
If Peter Piper picked a peck of pickled peppers,
Where's the peck of pickled peppers Peter Piper picked?

2. A big black bug bit a big black bear,
Made the big black bear bleed blood.

3. She sells sea shells by the sea shore.
The shells she sells are surely seashells.
So if she sells shells on the seashore,
I'm sure she sells seashore shells.

4. How much wood would a woodchuck chuck
if a woodchuck could chuck wood?
He would chuck, he would, as much as he could,
and chuck as much wood as a woodchuck would
if a woodchuck could chuck wood.

One-liners:
Toy boat. Toy boat. Toy boat.
Three free throws.
Knapsack straps.
A noisy noise annoys an oyster.
Fat frogs flying past fast.
Which wristwatches are Swiss wristwatches?
We surely shall see the sun shine soon.
Moose noshing much mush.
Black bug's blood.
Rubber baby buggy bumper.

Extension Ideas
✎ Have the children illustrate various tongue twisters.
✎ Write a book of tongue twisters. Children can either use already existing tongue twisters or write their own.
✎ Have tongue twister contests between various groups in your after-school program. Have them write tongue twisters that will stump the other groups.

"Content Standards"
Reading
Vocabulary and Concept Development
✎ Identify and sort common words in basic categories.
Phonemic Awareness
✎ Distinguish initial sounds in words.
✎ Create and state a series of rhyming words, including consonant blends.
Speaking Applications
✎ Recite poems, rhymes, songs, and stories.
Writing strategies
✎ Use descriptive words when writing.

Children's Books of Tongue Twisters
✎ *Busy Buzzing Bumblebees & Other Tongue Twisters,* **Alvin Schwartz**
✎ *Elmo's Tricky Tongue Twisters,* **Sarah Albee**
✎ *Giggle Fit: Tricky Tongue Twisters,* **Joseph Rosenbloom**
✎ *She Sells Seashells: A Tongue Twister Story,* **Grace Kim**
✎ *Six Sick Sheep: One Hundred One Tongue Twisters,* **Joanna Cole**

Great Websites for Tongue Twisters
Check out the websites listed on the website page in the back of the book for links. They have many other tongue twisters including ones in different languages.

Reproducible on p. 181

What's for Lunch?

Staff Role and Space

Staff will provide directions, support and supervision.
Comfortable writing area.

Time

Prep Time: Time to gather menus from the community, and find magazines for the children to use to cut out pictures.
Minimum Time Needed:
   45-minute session

Supplies

Examples of take-out menus
Construction paper
Clear contact paper or laminator
Magazines with pictures of food
Markers or crayons
Glue
Scissors

Adaptation/Modifications

✎ Help children who have difficulty with spelling refer to the sample menus for ideas of terms they can use on their menus.
✎ Have children dictate the words for their menu to a staff member who writes them down on a piece of paper. Then have the children copy the words onto their menu.
✎ Have the children make a menu completely out of pictures, then have the staff member write the term describing the picture underneath.

Purpose

To increase vocabulary and writing strategies including penmanship, organization and focus.

Directions

1. Share take out menus with children. Discuss different styles of menus, foods and everything included on the menus (foods, prices, pictures, etc.).

2. Provide children with magazines to cut out pictures of food and restaurant themes.

3. Encourage children to 'lay out' their menus so they can plan for what they will write before they glue the pictures on.

4. Assist children with planning their menus and spelling.

5. Have children glue pictures and write their menu items and prices. Drawing pictures adds creativity.

6. When menus are completed, cover in clear contact paper or laminate.

7. Use in your drama center for restaurant play!

> Psst ...
> Have a copy of the food pyramid handy for children to refer to so they create healthy menus.

Extension Ideas

✎ Laminate real take out menus to be used at your site so that the children may take their own menus home if they like.

✎ Be sure to encourage a variety of menus: Chinese, Fast Food, Fine Dining, etc.

✎ Plan a dinner or lunch for families and have the children make simple menus which include all that will be served!

✎ Create restaurant style chef hats, aprons and ordering pads for more fun.

✎ Let children help order a snack or meal from a restaurant using a real take-out menu.

"Content Standards"

Reading

Vocabulary and Concept Development

✎ Classify grade appropriate categories of words.

Writing

Writing Strategies

✎ Group related ideas and maintain a consistent focus.

✎ Create readable documents with legible handwriting.

Fun Literacy Activities for After-School Programs

Activities for Children
Ages Nine Through Ten
Transitional – Independent Readers

1. The activities match the developmental needs of the age of the children because each activity

   ✎ Takes some time to finish and requires some skill and patience,

   ✎ Encourages the participants to work together, and

   ✎ Is focused on their own lives and exploration of the world around them.

2. The activities match the reading, writing and speaking ability of most children at this age. At this age most children are at one of the following stages of literacy development:

   ✎ **Transitional:** They are able to read simple books and write simple narratives and descriptions.

   ✎ **Independent:** They continue to gain greater and greater fluency in reading and writing.

Unit Ideas

   ✎ **Drama Unit:** *Reader's Theater*

   ✎ **All About the Law Unit:** *Fairy Tale Characters on Trial*

   ✎ **Mystery Unit:** *Treasure Hunt, Secret Messages*

   ✎ **Movie Unit:** *Movie Posters*

Basketball Sentences

Staff Role and Space

Staff should provide support and supervision. Will need to prepare word cards.
Basketball court

Time

Prep Time: Could take up to an hour to make word cards, or, have older participants make them.
Minimum time needed:
    20 minutes

Supplies

Basketball
Word Card Set
    8 x 11.5 sheets preferably
    laminated, with individual words
    printed on them
Punctuation Cards— . , ! ?
Cards to designate the presence of a capital letter—i.e. **CAPITAL**

Adaptation/Modifications

✎ If the children have trouble initially coming up with their own sentences, the staff member can pre-select the words and the sentence that has to be formed. The staff member says the sentence and the children shoot until they can form it.
✎ If you have a physically challenged child who doesn't want to play, place that person in charge of arranging the word cards as instructed by the teams.

Purpose

To reinforce proper sentence structure and sight vocabulary.

Directions

1. Make a set of word cards. (Better yet, have the children make them.) The word cards should include many of the sight vocabulary words and other words that the children often use.

2. Have the children divide into even teams.

3. Place sets of cards near the basketball hoops.

4. Have each team member individually shoot a basket. If they make the basket, that individual gets to pick up a word from the pile.

5. The shooting continues until one team can make a sentence that makes sense and is as long as the number of individuals on the team, including the proper punctuation card and the card designating proper capitalization.

Added rules:
✎ The teams or the staff pre-determine how many words have to be in the sentence.
✎ Other restrictions can be made. For instance, the sentence has to be a question, or there has to be at least one adjective.

Psst...
You can start out in the beginning of the year with just a few word cards and build your sets through the year, increasing the difficulty of the words.

Fun Literacy Activities for After-School Programs

Variations

✎ The participants play HORSE, but instead of using the word HORSE they can use their spelling words. When they make a basket, they *get* a letter, instead of having a letter taken away. When they spell the word correctly, they win.

✎ Divide into relay teams. Each participant takes turns dribbling the ball down court, picking up a word and running back to form a sentence. The first team to make their sentence wins.

✎ If you cannot go outside, follow the same directions, but use garbage cans as your basket and thow "indoor" balls.

Examples of Word Cards

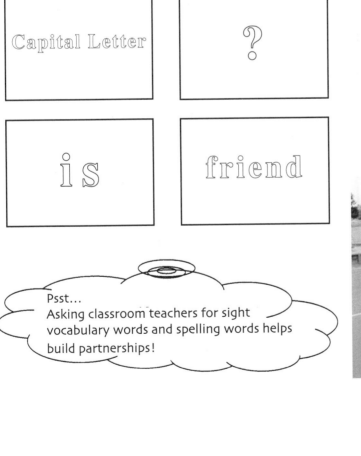

Psst...
Asking classroom teachers for sight vocabulary words and spelling words helps build partnerships!

Extension Ideas

✎ Hold Sentence Basketball tournaments.
✎ Have the participants write up the rules so other groups will know how to play.
✎ Have older children lead the younger children in the games.

"Content Standards"

Writing

Sentence Structure
✎ Write and speak in complete, coherent sentences.

Punctuation
✎ Use a period, exclamation point, or question mark at the end of sentences.

Capitalization
Capitalize the first word of a sentence.

9 to 10

Can You Save the Day?

Staff Role and Space

Staff will lead the discussion, read the book and then provide directions, support and supervision.

It's best to have a quiet area with few distractions and a table the children can use.

Time

Prep time: Time to collect magazines and other material
Minimum time needed:
Two 45-minute sessions:
  -10 minutes to introduce the activity
  -20 minutes to brainstorm ideas
  -15 minutes to read story
  -45 minutes for the activity

Supplies

Colored pencils and paper
Thesaurus and dictionary
Old magazines to cut up
Scissors and glue

Adaptation/Modifications

✎ Pair older children up with younger children for a fun buddy project!

Psst ...
Make sure to include as many heroines as heroes. Empower our girls!

Purpose

To encourage creative writing by asking children how they could save the day and having them make flyers about their plans.

Directions

1. Begin a discussion with the children about heroes and saving the day. Examples:
   a. "What does 'saving the day' mean to you?
   b. "Who are some of the heroes you know of? How do they save the day?"
   c. "How would you like to help others and save the day?"

2. Read a story in which the character performs a heroic act. Discuss the story and the hero's strengths.

3. Group brainstorm ideas of problems people may have and ways we can 'save the day' by helping them out.

4. Explain to the children that they will be creating a flyer to share with others on how they plan to save the day.

5. Provide children with scrap paper and have them make a rough draft of a picture and writing of how they would like to 'save the day'.

6. Have children peer proof each other's rough drafts.

7. Supply children with materials and support their creativeness!

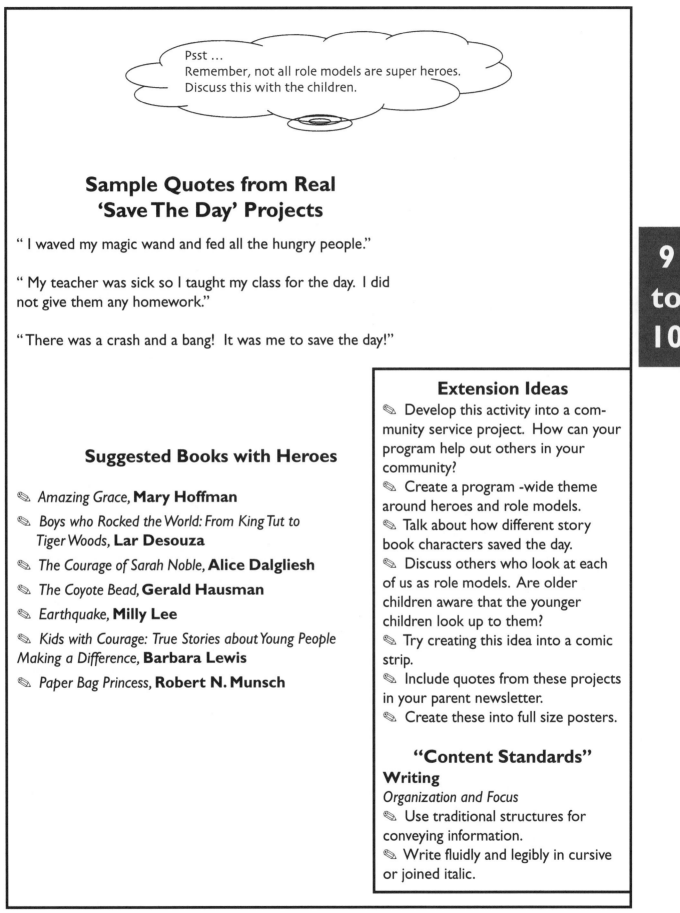

Psst …
Remember, not all role models are super heroes.
Discuss this with the children.

Sample Quotes from Real 'Save The Day' Projects

" I waved my magic wand and fed all the hungry people."

" My teacher was sick so I taught my class for the day. I did not give them any homework."

"There was a crash and a bang! It was me to save the day!"

Suggested Books with Heroes

- *Amazing Grace,* **Mary Hoffman**
- *Boys who Rocked the World: From King Tut to Tiger Woods,* **Lar Desouza**
- *The Courage of Sarah Noble,* **Alice Dalgliesh**
- *The Coyote Bead,* **Gerald Hausman**
- *Earthquake,* **Milly Lee**
- *Kids with Courage: True Stories about Young People Making a Difference,* **Barbara Lewis**
- *Paper Bag Princess,* **Robert N. Munsch**

Extension Ideas

- Develop this activity into a community service project. How can your program help out others in your community?
- Create a program -wide theme around heroes and role models.
- Talk about how different story book characters saved the day.
- Discuss others who look at each of us as role models. Are older children aware that the younger children look up to them?
- Try creating this idea into a comic strip.
- Include quotes from these projects in your parent newsletter.
- Create these into full size posters.

"Content Standards"
Writing
Organization and Focus
- Use traditional structures for conveying information.
- Write fluidly and legibly in cursive or joined italic.

Clap Those Hands!

Staff Role and Space

Staff should provide examples and lead initial discussion and provide support and supervision. Male role models are very effective to help encourage interest of all participants!
Can be done in any space.

Time

Prep Time: Copying the rhymes used for the games and time to gather material
Minimum time needed:
  30 minutes initially. This activity can be done anytime after initial introduction.

Supplies

Copies of rhymes used for hand-clapping games
Paper and pencils
Material for decorating copies of rhymes - markers, colored pencils (optional)

Adaptation/Modifications

✎ Hand clapping games have been traditionally "girls" games. If some of the boys are resistant, make sure they feel safe in doing the activity by making it clear that put-downs are unacceptable and that the area where you are doing the activity has some privacy.
✎ Talk to the physically challenged children in the program about how they want to be involved in this activity. Just because they have coordination problems does not mean they should be excluded from joining in.

Purpose

To increase awareness of the rhythm of language, and to develop phonemic awareness.

Directions

If you want to support the literacy aspect of this activity, make sure that you give the participants the songs and directions in written form instead of just orally and visually.

1. Give the participants a copy of the clapping song, "Long-legged Sailor." You will find a copy on page 182. Allow them to try to figure out how to sing the song and do the movements.

2. Practice the song with movements together until they have it mastered.

3. Give them copies of other songs that have traditionally been used for clapping games and have them come up with movements. Two traditional songs are given on the next page. Others can be found in the books listed as references.

4. Have them come up with movements and practice them to see if they work.

5. Brainstorm and write down on the board or chart paper phrases that describe the common movements that they are using.

6. Have them write down the directions for the movements so that other participants can follow them.

7. Have them exchange sheets and try following the directions.

Psst...
Once the children learn these games, they will be doing them everywhere. Be ready for the fun!

Miss Mary Mack

Miss Mary Mack, Mack, Mack,
All dressed in black, black, black,
With silver buttons, buttons, buttons,
All down her back, back, back.
She went upstairs to make her bed,
She made a mistake and bumped her head;
She went downstairs to wash the dishes,
She made a mistake and washed her wishes;
She went outside to hang her clothes,
She made a mistake and hung her nose.

Miss Lucy Had a Baby

Miss Lucy had a baby
She named him Tiny Tim
She put him in the bathtub
To see if he could swim.

He drank up all the water
He ate up all the soap.
He tried to eat the bathtub,
But it wouldn't go down his throat.

Miss Lucy called the doctor.
Miss Lucy called the nurse.
Miss Lucy called the lady
With the alligator purse.

In walked the doctor,
In walked the nurse,
In walked the lady
With the alligator purse.

"Measles," said the doctor.
"Chicken pox," said the nurse.
"Mumps," said the lady
With the alligator purse.

"Penicillin," said the doctor.
"Aspirin," said the nurse.
"Pizza," said the lady
With the alligator purse.

A dime for the doctor,
A nickel for the nurse,
Nothing for the lady
With the alligator purse.

Out walked the doctor,
Out walked the nurse,
Out walked the lady
With the alligator purse.

Suggested Resources

✎ *Hand Clap! "Miss Mary Mack" and 42 Other Hand Clapping Games for Kids*, **Sara Bernstein**

✎ *Miss Mary Mack and Other Children's Street Rhymes*, **Joanna Cole and Stephanie Calmenson**

Basic Clapping Pattern:

Clap your own hands together; clap your right hand against your partner's right hand; clap your own hands together; and clap your partner's left hand with your left hand.

Encourage the participants to get creative!!! For example:

✎ clapping outstretched hands palm to palm, hands facing up like holding a platter, one partner's palms facing down.

✎ clap the front of your own legs, sides of your own legs, knees

Extension Ideas

✎ There are many other kinds of movement activities including multicultural dances. Start out with the handclapping games and move into more complex activities.

✎ Have the children write one of the verses from a clapping game, and then decorate the picture.

✎ Make a mural out of the lyrics. Roll out a long piece of butcher paper or postal wrapping paper. Divide it into sections. Have pairs of children take a verse, write it and then draw a picture. Display the mural.

"Content Standards"

Great for remedial support in phonemic awareness.

Reading

Phonemic Awareness

✎ Track auditorily each word in a sentence and each syllable in a word.

Reading Comprehension

✎ Read narrative and expository text aloud with grade-appropriate fluency.

9 to 10

Reproducible on p. 182

Comic Strips By Us

Staff Role and Space

Staff should provide examples, lead initial discussion, provide support and supervise.
Table top space, or art activity area, is best for this activity.

Time

Prep Time: Gathering of materials, preparing comics and copying
Minimum Time Needed:
45 minute session
This is likely to become a program favorite and children may choose to participate as often as it is available.

Supplies

A large selection of comic strip samples
Pens and pencils
Erasers
White out
Dictionary and Thesaurus
A sense of humor

Adaptation/Modifications

✎ Staff or older children may assist younger children with spelling and writing as necessary. Have the child dictate what they want to have written for them.

Purpose

To convey humor through writing while creating comic strip dialogue, and to reinforce writing dialogue.

Prep

1. Collect a large selection of comic strips. Traditionally, Sunday newspapers have a great selection.

2. Divide comics into two folders:
   1. To share with the children and,
   2. To copy and distribute.

3. For the comics that will be distributed, white-out the original writing on the comic strip. This includes all dialogue.

4. Copy the whited-out comics. Make as many copies of various comics as participants you have.

Directions

1. Allow time for participants to read and enjoy a large variety of comic strip examples.

2. As a group, discuss favorite comic strips and why they are favorites. Include:
   ✎ favorite characters
   ✎ funny situations
   ✎ the style of the comic strip

3. Distribute the copied comic strips that have had the written words whited-out.

4. Explain to the children that they will add the writing to the comics. This may include narrative, explanation of scene and dialogue.

Psst ...
Set clear expectations with the participants about what type of humor is acceptable, and what is not.

Psst …
Creating large poster board size strips makes for great wall decorations!

5. Allow the participants enough time to be as creative as possible.

6. Suggest the use of a dictionary and a thesaurus to expand vocabulary and to check spelling.

Psst …
Begin with simple comics that do not require a lot of dialogue. This helps hesitant children enjoy the process!

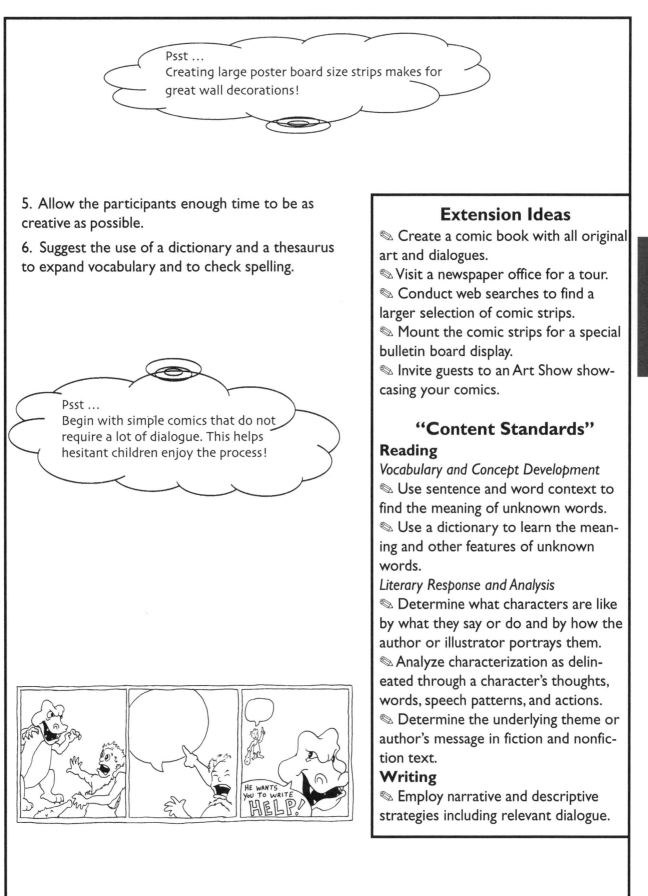

Extension Ideas
✎ Create a comic book with all original art and dialogues.
✎ Visit a newspaper office for a tour.
✎ Conduct web searches to find a larger selection of comic strips.
✎ Mount the comic strips for a special bulletin board display.
✎ Invite guests to an Art Show showcasing your comics.

"Content Standards"
Reading
Vocabulary and Concept Development
✎ Use sentence and word context to find the meaning of unknown words.
✎ Use a dictionary to learn the meaning and other features of unknown words.
Literary Response and Analysis
✎ Determine what characters are like by what they say or do and by how the author or illustrator portrays them.
✎ Analyze characterization as delineated through a character's thoughts, words, speech patterns, and actions.
✎ Determine the underlying theme or author's message in fiction and nonfiction text.
Writing
✎ Employ narrative and descriptive strategies including relevant dialogue.

9
to
10

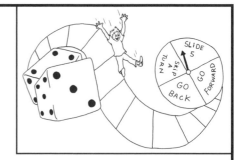

Create a Board Game

Staff Role and Space

Staff will give initial directions, support and supervision.
An art activity area, or tables and chairs.

Time

Prep Time: Time to gather supplies
Minimum Time Needed:
   Two 45-minute sessions
Depending on how elaborate the board games, children may need more sessions to complete their games. This is a great club project to expand over a few weeks.

Supplies

Board to record ideas
Colored file folders
Game piece markers (different colored buttons, coins, small toys, etc.)
Pens, markers, pencils, erasers
Rulers
Selection of board games
Magazines to cut up for pictures (optional)
Spinners (optional)
Poster board to make cards (optional)

Adaptation/Modifications

✎ Creating games that require no reading, such as Candyland®, may also be enouraged.
✎ Team children up in a way so that they can assist each other.

Purpose

For participants to develop, write and follow sequential directions through creating and sharing their own board games.

Directions

1. Gather participants and explain to them that they will be making their own board games. Have a selection of favorite board games to share and discuss.

2. Have the participants brainstorm ideas which may include:
   ✎ How different board games are set up;
   ✎ Which games are their favorites and why they are favorites;
   ✎ What are popular game pieces, directions and other things included with board games;
   ✎ Whether spinners, dice or other means of determining spaces moved are used; and
   ✎ How direction cards are used; what type of directions are written on them;
   ✎ What other topics could be used to make board games.

3. Participants may work individually or in groups to create their own board games.

4. Have participants plan, organize and make a rough 'draft' of their board game on scrap paper.

Psst ...
Keeping materials available at all times will help promote game making during free time!

Psst ...
Try collecting games made by the children to match the themes your program uses throughout the year!

Assembly Ideas

✎ Use colored file folders as boards. These allow for easy storage.

✎ Recycle spinners or dice from old games if needed.

✎ See below for ideas on boardgame space 'paths'.

✎ Tape an envelope to the back outside of the file folder to store cards and other pieces.

✎ Directions can be written directly on board game for easy reference.

Theme Ideas

Favorite Cartoons	Fairy Tales
These 50 States	Pets
Favorite Television Shows	Friends
The Food Pyramid	Nature
Favorite Books	Sports
Favorite Activities	Movies
A Day in the Life of	Zoo Animals

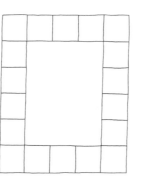

Extension Ideas

✎ Have Family Game night and invite friends and families to enjoy the new games.

✎ Have a Game Tournament.

✎ Contact a large department, variety, or toy store (Wal-Mart, Target) about a tour.

✎ Share your games with the local or school library.

✎ Take Polaroid pictures and use them on the game boards or creatively as game pieces.

✎ Make a huge 'life size' game on the play ground and participants actually move about as the game pieces.

"Content Standards"

Reading

Comprehension

✎ Follow multiple-step instructions in a basic technical manual.

Writing

Writing Strategies

✎ Include simple supporting facts and details.

Grammar

✎ Identify and use subjects and verbs correctly in speaking and writing simple sentences.

Evaluation and Revision

✎ Edit and revise selected drafts to improve coherence and progression by adding, deleting, consolidating, and rearranging text.

9 to 10

Dear Favorite...

Staff Role and Space

Staff will provide materials, assistance with research, supervision and encouragement. Comfortable writing area.

Time

Prep time: Time to gather materials and addresses for popular children's book authors. Older participants can do this through web-hunting.

Minimum time needed:

Time to explore books and authors to determine a favorite will vary based on the amount of exposure the children have to books.

45 minutes for the writing of the letter.

Supplies

Paper and envelopes
Computer access, or mailing addresses of authors
Pens, stickers, markers, etc.
Sample reading materials

Adaptation/Modifications

✎ Younger children can dictate a letter to an older child or adult.
✎ Encourage children to work together in small groups.
✎ Have a variety of age appropriate favorite books from the library displayed to encourage enthusiasm

Purpose

To provide children with an opportunity to creatively express their feelings while working on writing skills.

Directions

1. Discuss authors with children. Some ideas for the discussion are:

    a. What books has this author written?
    b. Does the author have a familiar theme or characters in the different books?
    c. Do you think this author relates to the characters in the book?

2. Tell the children that they will be writing letters to their favorite authors. They will discuss books, ask questions or tell about themselves in these letters.

3. Supply children with resources and materials necessary to write a rough draft letter.

4. Encourage children to proofread their letters. Peer edits are effective with this age group.

5. Have children write a final draft and address the envelope. A trip to the post office adds fun!

Psst ...
Notify your local children's librarian about this activity. The children may be able to share their responses with the community.

**Suggested Resource for
Author Contact**
A www.yahoo.com or www.google.com
search for children's authors will provide the
children with many hits of author's web pages
which often include postal addresses and a lot
of information.

Dear J.K. Rowling,

     I really enjoyed Harry Potter and the Order of the Phoenix. But, I wanted to ask you, was the writing of it fun? Hard? My favorite characters are Tonk, Harry and Mad Eyes. I am interested to know if you are going to write a sixth, seventh, or even eighth Harry Potter book?
     Good luck writing and I give you 20 million Fire Bolt thumbs up!

Sincerely,

Zachary Edwards
Your #1 fan!

Psst ...
Provide children with brightly colored paper and a variety of supplies to encourage creativity. Rubber stamps, glitter, markers, etc.

Extension Ideas

✎ Have children create posters or bulletin board displays with their favorite authors books, letters and responses to share.
✎ Have children copy their letters and bind them all together for everyone to share.
✎ Children can report in the monthly newsletter about this project and any responses they receive from the authors.
✎ Check in with the local library and bookstores for visiting authors.

"Content Standards"
Writing
Write Responses to Literature
✎ Demonstrate an understanding of the literary work.
✎ Support judgments through references to both the text and prior knowledge.

9
to
10

Do I Have a Dream for You!

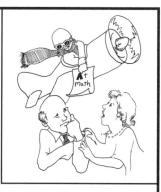

Staff Role and Space

Staff should lead initial discussion and provide support and supervision. Can be done in any space.

Time

Prep Time: Time to gather material and make copies of the speech outline

Minimum time needed:
Two 45-minute sessions. This activity could take longer if the participants make visual aids.

Supplies

Index cards
Scrap paper
Pencil/Pens
Tag board (optional)
Markers (optional)
Speaker's Podium , i.e. cardboard box (optional)

Adaptation/Modifications

✎ For children who have difficulty speaking in front of groups, team them up with more confident children. Have them present their speech together so that the child does not feel so vulnerable.
✎ For bilingual children, allow them to give their talks in the language they are most comfortable with.

Purpose

To practice speaking in front of others and learn how to develop a persuasive argument.

Directions

1. Ask the children to individually write down five things that they enjoy doing. Tell them that the things they write down can not be illegal, profane or harmful in any way towards themselves or others.

2. Divide the participants into groups of three. Ask them to read their lists to each other.

3. Have them brainstorm a job that would suit their interests. They might not be able to include all their interests, but encourage them to include as many as they can. The sillier the better.

> *For instance, for a person who likes sports, people, good money and the outdoors, their job could be a "bungee jumping instructor."*

4. Have each person in the group think of at least four reasons their parents should help them pay for the training for their chosen job. Have them write one reason on four different index cards.

5. Have them talk with the rest of their group about their ideas and have everyone brainstorm possibly better ideas. Remind them they have to come up with ideas that will convince their parents, not their friends.

Psst...
Children get easily bored, (and so do the adults) if they have to listen to speeches one after another. If you have a large group, split them up, and have them present to their smaller group.

6. Following the outline provided, have them prepare a one to three minute talk. Tell them **not** to write out the whole speech. Have them jot down phrases instead of sentences.

7. Have them give their speeches to their fellow participants. The participants should pretend they are parents, and tell the speaker whether they have been convinced or not.

An Example:

> Likes to eat
>
> Listening to music
>
> Playing with friends
>
> Watching TV
>
> Sleep

Ideal Job: *Running a Café for Couch Potatoes*

Speech Outline

(Available as handout on p. 183)

Position Statement: The job that I would like is _____. I would like you to help me by_____.

Reason:
_____

Explanation:

Reason:
_____

Explanation:

Reason:
_____

Explanation:

Conclusion:

Extension Ideas

✎ Ask parents to come in and listen to the speeches. Have them provide feedback to the speakers about what worked and did not work in their speeches.

✎ Have the participants develop visual aids to use in their speeches.

✎ Have a business person come in and discuss how presentations are used in his or her work. Invite a member of Toastmasters to visit and share public speaking experiences.

✎ Take controversial topics and have the participants come up with arguments to persuade others to their point of view.

✎ Have children develop a PowerPoint presentation to go along with their talk.

"Content Standards"
Listening and Speaking
Organization and Delivery of Oral Communication

✎ Select a focus, organizational structure, and point of view for an oral presentation.

✎ Clarify and support spoken ideas with evidence and examples.

Reproducible on p. 183

9 to 10

Fairy Tale Characters on Trial

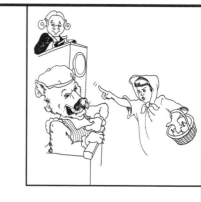

Staff Role and Space

Staff leads discussion and supports planning. May participate in trial.
Enough room for small groups to plan, "Court room" area with room for a judge, lawyers and jury.

Time

Prep Time: The staff will have to take time to familiarize themselves with the mechanics of trials and decide on an appropriate fairy tale.

Minimum time needed

Depending on how elaborate you want to be:
- 45-minute session to talk about trials, and read the fairy tale
- 45-minute session to develop strategies for the trial (arguments, witnesses, evidence displays)
- 45-minute session for the trial

Supplies

Book of fairy tales
Evidence displays (optional):
    Chart paper or White board
    Markers
Prop Ideas (optional):
    Cardboard box podium
    Judges' robe
    Briefcase

Adaptation/Modifications

✎ Have the participants choose which role in the trial they want to play, allowing shyer children to take smaller roles.

✎ Children can try out for the different roles.

Purpose

To be able to organize material, and to practice public speaking.

Directions

1. Talk about court room trials. Ideas that you can discuss include
    ✎ Why do we have trials?
    ✎ What are plaintiffs, defendants, judges, lawyers, juries, witnesses?
    ✎ What is evidence?

2. Tell them that they are going to put a fairy tale character on trial.

3. Read a fairy tale. (Check out fairy tales from other countries.)

4. Decide on the character you are going to put on trial. For example,
    ✎ The wolf in "The Three Little Pigs"
    ✎ The witch in "Hansel and Gretel"
    ✎ The stepmother in "Cinderella"

5. Talk and come up with
    ✎ Arguments to defend the character,
    ✎ Arguments to convict the character,
    ✎ Evidence that they can use,
    ✎ Witnesses that they can call.

6. Choose a judge, defendant, plaintiff, lawyers, and witnesses.

7. Conduct the trial.

Psst ...
Bring in another group of kids or parents to be the jury.

Hints for Preparing for the Trial

1. Set up the room to look like a courtroom.

2. Work together to decide on the charges.

3. Have the kids work in teams – the defense team and the plaintiff team.

4. Have the teams come up with the witnesses they want to call and the questions they will ask.

5. Encourage children to come up with sentencing suggestions before the trial. The sillier the sentence, the more fun.

6. Have the jury come up with both a guilty and a non-guilty verdict giving reasons for both.

Suggested Resources for Fairy Tales

✎ *Multicultural Fables and Fairy Tales,* **Tara McCarthy**

✎ *The Golden Book of Fairy Tales (Golden Classics),* **Marie Ponsot**

✎ *Don't Bet on the Prince: Contemporary Feminist Fairy Tales in North America and England,* **Jack Zipes**

✎ *Fairy Tales,* **Berlie Doherty**

Resources for Reader's Theater

✎ *12 Fabulously Funny Fairy Tale Plays,* Scholastic Press

✎ *Multicultural Folktales: Readers Theatre for Elementary Students,* **Suzanne I. Barchers**

See Websites listed at the back of the book for links to fairy tales online.

Extension Ideas

✎ Write the summation speeches for both sides.

✎ Visit a courtroom.

✎ Have a judge or lawyer come and talk to the participants.

✎ Have a parent who was on a jury come in and talk about his or her experience.

✎ Perform plays based on fairy tales. For example you could perform "The True Story of the Three Little Pigs" by Jon Scieszka. Check the website suggestions found in the back of the book for a script.

"Content Standards"

Reading

Narrative Text: Elements of a story

✎ Identifying characters.

✎ Comparing and contrasting characters.

Vocabulary Development

Written and Oral English-Language Conventions

✎ Use complete and correct declarative, interrogative, imperative and exclamatory sentences in writing and speaking.

Listening and Speaking

✎ Retelling stories, using characters, plot, setting.

✎ Make narrative presentations that relate ideas, observations, or recollections about events and provide a context and insight.

9 to 10

Fortunately/ Unfortunately Cookies

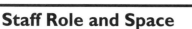

Staff Role and Space

Staff should lead project and provide support and supervision. Staff may decide to cut the strips of paper in advance. Kitchen area with oven necessary.

Time

Prep Time: Time to gather materials
Minimum time needed:

   -30 minutes for explanation and Fortunately/Unfortunately strip making

   -45 minutes for baking and folding cookies.

Supplies

Strips of paper the size of fortunes in fortune cookies, pens, scissors
Ingredients listed in the recipe
Non-stick cookie sheets
Oven mitts
Measuring cups and spoons
Wire whisk
Spatula
2 Bowls, one large

Adaptation/Modifications

✎ Proficient writers may choose to write all of the 'fortunes' and other children may do all of the baking.

✎ English language learners may write in their native language. An adult or another child may translate the information onto the other side of the strip in English.

✎ Older children can look up definitions in their dictionaries.

✎ Use other words to replace fortunately and unfortunately.

Purpose

For children to work with contrasting concepts, specifically *fortunately* and *unfortunately*, while integrating cooking and language arts.

Directions

1. Explain to the children that they will be writing sentences using the words FORTUNATELY and UNFORTUNATELY on small strips of paper that they will bake inside cookies.

2. Display the definition of *Fortunately* and *Unfortunately* on the board or a large flip chart of paper.

3. Brainstorm examples of sentences using *fortunately* and *unfortunately*. Write a few down as examples, using the following format:

      Fortunately: it is fortunate that...

      Unfortunately: it is unfortunate that...

4. As a group, pick a story line that lends itself to many fortunate and unfortunate events. A few examples include:

   - We bought a new kitty. **Fortunately**, he is very cute. **Unfortunately**, he scratched up all our furniture.

   - I rode my bike across town. **Fortunately**, it was a sunny day. **Unfortunately**, I got a flat tire.

5. Once a story line is agreed upon, divide the children into equal groups of 'fortunatelys' and 'unfortunatelys.' All the *fortunatelys* will write a fortunate sentence on a strip of paper and *unfortunatelys* will write an unfortunate sentence on their strip of paper.

6. When the strips are all written, set them to the side and wash hands for cookie making.

7. Use the following recipe and directions for the cookies. A reproducible page is found on page 184.

8. When cookies are ready to eat, sit in a group and share the FORTUNATELYS and UNFORTUNATELYS out loud for a lot of giggles and laughs.

Cookie Recipe

- Preheat oven to 325°
- Ingredients: 1/2 cup flour   1/3 cup sugar
  1/2 tsp. salt   1 Tbsp. cornstarch
  4 egg whites   2 Tbsp milk
  1/4 cup melted butter or margarine
  2 tsp. almond extract
- Combine flour, sugar, cornstarch and salt.
- In a separate bowl, beat butter, egg whites, milk and almond extract until smooth.
- Drop dough by tablespoons, 3 inches apart, onto greased cookie sheets.
- Bake 9-10 minutes, or until golden brown, on middle oven rack.
- Remove from cookie sheet immediately with spatula, onto waxed paper.
- Immediately, set one FORTUNATELY or UNFORTUNATELY strip of paper in center of each cookie.
- Without hesitating, fold each cookie in half and press edges to seal. (Fig. 1)
- Fold warm cookie over the edge of a clean bowl and hold for approximately 20 seconds to set shape. (Fig. 2)
- Let cookies cool.

Extension Ideas

✎ Make special occasion cookies with fortunes or announcements proper for the occasion.

✎ Have the children write their names on the slips and track who gets the cookie they made.

✎ Write opening story sentences on the strips and have the children verbally complete the story when they open the cookie.

✎ Visit a bakery and ask for a tour of their kitchen area.

✎ Invite families to share different desserts their families enjoy.

"Content Standards"
Written Language
Sentence Structure

✎ Use simple and compound sentences in writing.

✎ Use transitions and conjunctions to connect ideas.

Fig. 1

Fig. 2

Psst...
The cookies must be folded very quickly while they are still warm. You will be more successful if you cook a few at a time and fold quickly.

Reproducible on p. 184

9 to 10

Grab Bag Demos — Beyond Show & Tell

Staff Role and Space

The staff will prepare the demonstration topics and provide direction and supervision. Prepare the demo choices on strips of paper and put them in a bag.
The space is adaptable to work with the topics of the presentations. For instance, a cooking demonstration will need to be in the kitchen area.

Time

Prep Time: Time to gather materials for grab bags
Minimum time needed:
   Two 45-minute sessions:
      Discussion and preparing demos
      Actual presentations

Supplies

Strips of paper with demonstration ideas written on them
Paper bag
Flip chart paper, poster board, a chalk board or a white board
Specific props and supplies as needed for individual demos

Adaptation/Modifications

✎ Shy children may prefer to buddy up and assist another child in a presentation.
✎ Allow children to present in their home language.
✎ Try a demonstration without speaking.

Purpose

For children to organize information and practice speaking in front of a group.

Directions

Staff Prep

1. Before gathering children together, prepare strips of paper with presentation/demo ideas and drop them into a bag for children to pick out. Be sure to only include ideas that are feasible for the children to complete. Consider time, supplies, talents and space availability. Or, you may decide to let children choose their own topics.

2. Set up centers with the supplies for each of the demos in the bag. Also, provide materials for them to write and draw on for their presentation.

Activity

1. Discuss with children what presentations are. You may include in your discussion:

   ✎ Teachers often give presentations when they are showing students a new skill.

   ✎ Ask the children if their parents give presentations at work.

   ✎ Presentations are often called demonstrations.

   ✎ Sometimes people use computers in their presentations.

Psst...
This activity can be as involved or as spontaneous as you would like it to be. With preparation, time and supplies, this may turn into quite a production!

> Psst...
> When children are nervous speaking in front of the group, remind them, "Practice is what tames the butterflies."

✎ Cooking shows use presentations to show the viewers how to cook special recipes.

✎ On airplanes, flight attendants give presentations on showing passengers how to use the seat belts and what to do in emergencies.

2. Tell the children they will have the opportunity to make a presentation to their friends in a fun, relaxed way.

3. Pair the children up and have each pair pick a strip of paper out of the bag. This is the demo they will present.

4. Provide children the time and materials to prepare their demos.

5. Tell the children how long they have to prepare for their presentation, and how long their presentation should be. For instance, they will have 20 minutes to prepare a two minute presentation.

6. Encourage the children to use posters or other large writing areas to show pictures, basic information and pictures of interests.

7. Have the pairs of children give their presentations.

Grab Bag Demo Ideas

1. Paper Bag Presto! Now a Book Cover!
2. Peanut Butter Sandwich Delights
3. The History of M&M's
4. Baseball Basics
5. French Braiding for Beginners
6. Hand Clapping Games
7. Tying a Shoe
8. Preparing a Scrapbook Page

Extension Ideas

✎ Invite the families for a night of Presentation Demonstrations so the children can present their demonstrations.

✎ Invite a professional trainer or presenter to visit and give the children tips on presenting.

✎ Try other forms of improvisational theater games.

✎ For a field trip, go to a local live theater show.

✎ Make this a long term project and encourage the children to learn how to make Power Point presentations.

"Content Standards"
Listening and Speaking
Comprehension

✎ Summarize major ideas and supporting evidence presented in spoken messages and formal presentations.
Organization and Delivery of Oral Communication

✎ Use details, examples, anecdotes, or experiences to explain or clarify information.

✎ Emphasize points in ways that help the listener or viewer to follow important ideas and concepts.

Suggested Resource Books
Fiction
✎ *The Great Show and Tell Disaster,* **Mike Reiss**
Non-Fiction
✎ *Creating E-Reports and Online Presentations,* **Gary Souter**
✎ *Show and Tell (Real Kids Readers),* **Susan Hood**
✎ *Effective Presentation Skills: A Practical Guide for Better Speaking,* **Steve Mandel**

9 to 10

Mail Call!

Staff Role and Space

Staff should provide instruction to children on appropriate letter writing style and conventions. Also, encourage letter writing on a regular basis.

Can be done in any space, but best if participants can work at tables.

Time

Prep Time: Time to gather materials
Minimum time needed:

45 minutes for first session, and periodically throughout the year.

Supplies

Different types of writing paper
Pencils and pens
Box as big or bigger than a shoe box
Materials to decorate the box
Large appliance box to decorate as a regular size mailbox (optional)
Stenciling and other design material to make letterheads (optional)

Adaptation/Modifications

✎ Children who have difficulty composing a letter can write shorter messages and illustrate their ideas.
✎ Pair children up with writing buddies who will work together to compose letters.
✎ Allow children to write in their home language.

Purpose

To practice writing and sharing ideas with friends.

Directions

1. Talk to the children about sending and receiving letters. You might read one of the books suggested in the resources to get them thinking.

2. Introduce the idea of a program Post Office.

3. Allow the children to generate the rules and policies for the Post Office including:

> ✎ How and when the mail is going to be collected and delivered
> ✎ Privacy and sharing issues
> ✎ Consequences for inappropriate language/content or hurtful messages
> ✎ Whether anonymous letters can be sent

4. Let children make the mailbox they are going to use.

5. Initially have the children draw names for their penpal. Give them a theme for their first letter, like their favorite food, TV show, sport; what they hate, what they like.

6. Have a large chart with the proper form for writing informal letters. (See the format on the next page.)

7. Encourage the participants to write letters to each other throughout the year. Have regular mail calls during the year.

Make letter writing a regular part of your program requiring the children to write at least two letters a month. This is especially important if you team up with another site.

> Psst...
> Letter writing is a great quiet activity for children to do after they have finished their homework.

> Psst...
> Make sure that all children are getting some letters. If a child does not seem to be getting any, you can write to them or encourage a kind-hearted child to write one.

Letter Format

[Date: Month, Day, Year]

Dear _____,

[Message]

Yours truly,

[Signature]

Envelope Format

[Your name]   stamp
[Address]
[City, State, Zip Code]

    [Friend's name]
    [Their Address]
    [City, State, Zip Code]

Safety Rules for Exchanging E-mail Letters

1. Only tell your first name.

2. Do not give out personal information such as your last name, home address, parent's work address, or telephone number.

3. Never share a password for an Internet game or chat room with the online key pal.

4. Never agree to meet in person, especially alone, with someone you met online.

5. Notify the teacher and/or parent if you receive an obscene message.

6. Never send identifying pictures to your key pal. Class pictures are fine to send as long as individuals are not named (for example, John is the third person in the second row).

7. Never attach pictures or other files to an e-mail message unless the people receiving the message have given you permission.

Extension Ideas

✎ Have the children make their own letterhead stationery. Use stencils, print blocks or other decorating material.

✎ If exchanging letters with another group, make a video of your group doing different activities and saying hi to their letter-writing buddies. This activity works even better if your exchange group lives in another part of the country.

✎ Visit a post office and take a tour.

✎ Study stamps from different countries, and start a group stamp collection.

✎ Start an e-mail exchange, following the same procedure as the regular mail activity. See safety rules on this page.

"Content Standards"
Writing Application
✎ Write personal and formal letters, thank-you notes and invitations including the date, proper salutation, body, closing, and signature.
Written English Conventions
✎ Write with a command of standard English conventions including sentence structure, punctuation, capitalization, and spelling.

Suggested Resources
✎ *Where Does the Mail Go?: A Book About the Postal System,* Melvin Berger, Gilda Berger

✎ *Sending a Letter,* Alex Stewart

✎ *Abraham Lincoln: Letters from a Slave Girl (Dear Mr. President),* Andrea Davis Pinkney

✎ *Dear Children of the Earth: A Letter from Home,* Schim Schimmel
Fiction
✎ *Dear Juno,* Soyung Pak, Susan Kathleen Hartung

9 to 10

Movie Posters

Staff Role and Space

Staff will provide directions, supervision and enthusiasm.

A gym floor, or other large floor area, is best for children to spread out and be creative.

Time

Prep Time: Time to gather materials
Minimum time needed:
   45-minute session
(If you are going to read a book first, you will need another 45-minute session to read and discuss.)

Supplies

Large poster boards
Markers, crayons or colored pencils
Movie poster examples, current teen
   magazines, video covers

Adaptation/Modifications

✎ Encourage group projects to promote teamwork so every one can add their special touch and talents.

Purpose

For children to explore characters and plot through the use of creative writing and through artistic expression.

Directions

1. Discuss favorite movies and books with children. Sample discussion starters:

   a. Has your favorite book been made into a movie? If not, would you like it to be?

   b. What information is included on movie posters?

   c. What actress/actor would you like to see play your favorite characters?

2. Check out current movie posters or video tape covers for examples of information to include on posters.

3. Have the children select a book that has not been made into a movie. Explain that they are going to design a movie poster for their book.

4. (optional) Read a book that the group selects after talking about many different ones.

5. If the posters are going to be made for a contest, explain to children how they will be displayed.

6. Provide children with supplies and step back and enjoy their creativeness!

Psst ...
Check with local copy centers for poster board donations. If the posters are to be displayed in a public space, mention the name of the company that donated the posters.

Psst …
Encourage children to cover their poster board completely. This makes posters more polished!

Suggested Books
Short books that are of interest to 9-10 year olds

- ✎ *The Fortune-Tellers*, **Lloyd Alexander**
- ✎ *Raising Dragons*, **Jerdine Nolen**
- ✎ *Bad Case of Stripes*, **David Shannon**
- ✎ *Chato's Kitchen*, **Gary Soto**
- ✎ *How to Live Forever*, **Colin Thompson**
- ✎ *Golem*, **David Wisniewski**

Extension Ideas
✎ Ask the local movie theatre to display your movie posters.

✎ Check out movie web sites for poster examples and ideas of information to include.

✎ Have a poster contest to advertise your summer program. Ask the local library, school district, grocery store, etc. to display entries.

✎ On a smaller scale, children can create book covers for favorite books and stories.

✎ Children can create a bulletin board decorated as a movie poster.

✎ Instead of a movie poster, how about a live theatre production poster?

✎ Current teen magazines can provide examples, ideas for actors, etc.

"Content Standards"
Reading
Narrative analysis
✎ Use knowledge of the situation and setting and of character's traits and motivations to determine causes for the character's actions.
Writing Strategies
Organization and Focus
✎ Describe setting and plot.
Evaluation and revision
✎ Edit and revise to improve focus.

Musical Art

Staff Role and Space

The staff will prepare the activity area, provide directions and supervision.
Your art or painting area, or area where it is okay to be messy.

Time

Prep Time: Time to gather materials
Minimum time needed:
Two 45-minute sessions
  - One session for introduction and painting (need time for the paint to dry).
  - One session for the finishing work.

Supplies

Large sheets of painting paper
Paint & paint brushes, bold markers
Music – classical, jazz, rock, rap – a large variety
CD or tape player

Adaptation/Modifications

✎ Some children may hesitate to keep their eyes closed. This is fine and they should be encouraged to keep enjoying the activity.
✎ Younger children may choose to dictate their writings to an older child or an adult.

Purpose

For children to express themselves through painting and creative writing while being inspired by music and lyrics.

Directions

1. Have children positioned in front of their painting materials.

2. Turn on the music and instruct the children to close their eyes. It is recommended that you begin with soft, relaxing music.

3. In a soft, encouraging voice, ask the children to think about the following questions while they paint (No need for them to answer out loud):

> ✎ How does the music makes you feel?

> ✎ What do you see with your eyes shut? Can you picture the music?

> ✎ How would you express your feelings through words and painting?

4. Instruct the children to pick up their paint brushes and begin painting with their eyes still closed. They should try to paint the music, whatever they see and feel.

Psst...
With classical music, this can be a very relaxing and soothing transitional activity. It is a great activity for the end of the day when parents are picking up the children.

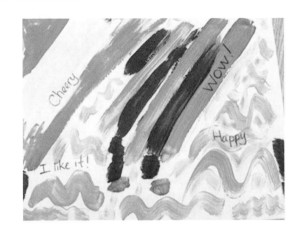

5. While the paint is drying, have the children write how they felt while listening to the music. If you listened to music without lyrics, the children may choose to write lyrics. Or, they may write poetry or a short story.

6. When the paint is dry, have the children edit and transform their writings on the paintings with bold markers. They may also choose to include the name of the piece of music as a title, or make up one of their own.

7. Mount the art work on heavy construction paper or mats for displaying.

8. Display these creative expressions and invite families to view and enjoy them.

Extension Ideas

✎ Visit a local artist gallery and ask the artist questions about inspiration.

✎ Attend a high school band concert. Ask about the different instruments and styles of music.

✎ Introduce a large variety of music. Ask children to notice the difference in their writings and art work that the different music inspires.

✎ Host an art exhibit evening. This may even be a fundraising auction!

"Content Standards"
Writing Strategies
Organization and Focus
✎ Use traditional structures for conveying information.
Evaluation and Revision
✎ Edit and revise selected drafts to improve coherence.

Psst...
After experimenting with this activity a few times, the children will be more comfortable and creative with their expressions.

Personalized Greeting Cards

Staff Role and Space

Staff will provide supervision and enthusiasm.

Comfortable writing and craft area.

Time

Prep Time: Time to gather materials
Minimum time needed:

45 minutes —

  5 minutes to introduce
 10 minutes to demonstrate skills
 30 minutes for the activity

Supplies

Colored pencils and paper
Thesaurus and dictionary
Old magazines and greeting cards to cut up
Scissors and glue
Stickers, rubber stamps, glitter, etc.
Envelopes

Adaptation/Modifications

✎ Buddy up children who have difficulty writing with fluent writers.
✎ Encourage English learners to create cards in their home language.

Purpose

To encourage creative writing and practice of written language conventions.

Directions

1. Discuss the purpose of greeting cards with the children. Share examples of different types of greeting cards, Birthday, Valentine's Day, Mother's Day, etc.

2. Explain to the children that they will be creating greeting cards and writing sentiments to give to their families and friends.

3. Demonstrate to children how to address an envelope. Provide an example on the table to share. (See an example in the Mail Call Activity on page 90).

4. As a group, brainstorm words children may want to include in their cards. Write these words on a large sheet of paper, or board to help children with spelling.

5. Help younger children fold their paper into cards. Folding a 8" x 11" sheet of paper in half twice makes a great size and shape for a card.

6. Assist the children, relax and enjoy their efforts!

Psst …
Receiving a card for 'no particular reason' is a very special treat. Brighten the parents' day by having the children slip them a 'just because' card.

Dear Annabelle,
I hope you have a fantastic birthay! And have a great day enjoy all your presents & friends! I love you so much!!!
Love always - Candace

Extension Ideas

✎ Copy special cards the children have made and have them personalize and deliver them to senior citizen homes in your community.

✎ Bundled sets of 4-10 cards, wrapped in brightly covered ribbons, make great fundraiser items to sell.

✎ Be sure to make cards for the diverse holidays and special events celebrated by the families in your community.

✎ Extra cards, such as thank you cards, can be kept on hand to be used by children and staff members at the spur of the moment.

✎ Use dried flowers to create beautiful spring cards.

"Content Standards"
Writing Strategies

✎ Students write clear sentences and paragraphs that develop a central idea.

✎ Showing consideration of audience and purpose.

Written Language Conventions

✎ Students write and speak with a command of standard English.

✎ Spell correctly.

✎ Use good penmanship.

9 to 10

Pet Rocks

Staff Role and Space

Staff should lead initial discussion and provide support and supervision.
Initial part of the activity will be done outside. Finishing the project will require writing at tables and a craft area.

Time

Prep Time: Time to gather materials
Minimum time needed:
   45-minute session

Supplies

Index cards
Rocks
Cotton
Wiggly eyes
Hot glue gun
Shoe boxes or smaller boxes
Paper, small note pads
Pencils or pens
Yarn

Adaptation/Modifications

✎ Younger children may draw pictures of their rocks instead of writing words to describe them.
✎ Pair older children up with the younger ones to create Pet Rock Buddies!

Purpose

For children to practice using descriptive words while engaged in careful observation of nature.

Directions

1. Enjoy a rock collecting adventure with the children. Encourage the children to collect rocks of different shapes and textures. The rocks should be able to fit in the palm of their hands.

2. When together as a group, explain that the children will be making a Pet Rock and a home for the Pet Rock.

3. Have the children share what is special about their rocks: Are there any special shapes? Colors? Textures?

4. Have the children write down the name of their rock on an index card with at least three specific and creative things about their rock. Encourage them to be as creative as possible with this activity. Silly descriptions work best. For example:

My Rock, Flying Heart
✎ *My rock has super powers and can fly through the air.*
✎ *My rock fits in my hand perfectly so that it can hide.*
✎ *My rock is shaped like a heart because it is so sweet.*

Psst...
 If you are unable to go rock collecting near your program, ask a landscape material company to donate rocks for the activity. The children can write the donation request and a thank you card.

Psst...
Warm the rocks on a cookie sheet in a 350 degree oven for 10 minutes. When the children use crayons on warm rocks, the crayon melts on thick and will not rub off! This is a great activity for a cold day. <u>Please supervise closely when heating rocks.</u>

5. The children now glue their index cards onto boxes. The children may decide to decorate the outside of the boxes with colorful paper and more writings.

6. The boxes will be the Rocks' homes. Line the boxes by gluing down cotton on the inside bottom.

7. Next, the children may add 'life' to their Rocks by gluing on wiggly eyes, coloring them and adding yarn for hair.

8. When the Rocks are completely decorated and dry, children may glue them down in their boxes.

9. Display Pet Rocks and their homes for parents to enjoy.

Suggested Resources

✎ *Smithsonian Handbooks: Rocks & Minerals (Smithsonian Handbooks)*, **Chris Pellant**

✎ *DK Handbooks: Rocks and Minerals*, **Cally Hall, Harry Taylor**

✎ *Eyewitness: Rocks & Minerals*, **R. F. Symes**

✎ *Rocks, Fossils and Arrowheads (Take-Along Guide)*, **Laura Evert**

✎ *Backpack Books: 1,001 Facts about Rocks & Minerals (Backpack Books)* **Sue Fuller.**

Extension Ideas

✎ Read the book *Everybody Needs a Rock,* **Byrd Baylor** to start the activity.

✎ Begin a rock collecting club.

✎ Children may write a script and film their Pet Rocks in action. These short films are often hilarious!

✎ Create Pet Rock journals in shapes of rocks with construction paper covers. Children can write stories and adventures of their Pets.

✎ Have children type up short stories about their Rocks and add pictures. Collect them and create a book for your program!

"Content Standards"
Writing
Writing Applications
✎ Relate ideas, observations, or recollections of an event or experience.
✎ Provide a context to enable the reader to imagine the world of the event or experience.
✎ Use concrete sensory details.
Written Language Conventions
✎ Write with a command of standard English conventions in penmanship, punctuation, spelling and capitalization.

9 to 10

Reader's Theater

Staff Role and Space

Staff initially should play the role of director until the children become more comfortable with the process.

Any space, but best if there is an open space that can act as a stage.

Time

Prep Time: Time to select and copy scripts and gather other material

Minimum time needed:
One 45-minute session, or up to a week's worth of activity time.

Supplies

Reader's scripts (check suggested resources for scripts)
Highlighters
Construction paper
String
Markers
Simple props based on the needs of the script (optional)

Adaptation/Modifications

✎ Assign the different roles in the play based on reading capability. The longer roles can be given to children who are more fluent readers. If children who have difficulty want a longer part, make sure to provide them with the opportunity to practice.

✎ Choose scripts that are age appropriate.

✎ Look for scripts that reflect the ethnicity of your children.

Purpose

To increase reading fluency and enjoyment of reading.

Directions

1. Select a script from the various resources on the next page and copy enough for each child who will be in the play.

2. Either the staff selects roles or the children decide. Have them highlight their part with a marker.

3. As a group, read through the play once to get the idea of the story.

4. Discuss the plot and the characters, and have the children decide how they should play the part based on the personality and actions of the character.

> For example, a mean character might have a low, harsh voice.

5. Write the name of the character on construction paper, and hang it around the neck of the child who is playing that character.

6. Practice the play enough times so the children are able to say their lines fluently.

Psst...
Many of the scripts for Reader's Theater are based on books. Read the children the book before they start working on the play so they get an idea of the plot and characters.

Hints for Reader's Theater

✎ At the beginning of the play have all children seated on stools facing the audience. If they move during their speaking parts have them return to their stools between lines.

✎ Remind the children that if they do move around as part of the role, they should look out to the audience while talking.

✎ Do not have the children memorize their lines. Part of the fun of reader's theater is the freedom from worrying about forgetting lines.

✎ Support the children to get into character by helping them change their voice tone, and if desired to wear simple costumes.

✎ Remember it is not the quality of the **performance** that is important, but the quality of the **fun**.

Suggested Books

✎ *12 Fabulously Funny Fairy Tale Plays,* **Justin McCory Martin**

✎ *Classic Readers Theatre for Young Adults,* **Suzanne I. Barchers, Jennifer L. Kroll** (For middle school and high school students.)

✎ *Fifty Fabulous Fables: Beginning Readers Theatre* **Suzanne I. Barchers**

✎ *Frantic Frogs and Other Frankly Fractured Folktales for Readers Theatre,* **Anthony D. Fredericks**

✎ *Just-Right Plays: 25 Emergent Reader Plays Around the Year (Grades K-1),* **Carol Pugliano, Carol Pugliano-Martin**

✎ *Multicultural Folktales: Readers Theatre for Elementary Students,* **Suzanne I. Barchers**

✎ *Readers Theatre for Beginning Readers,* **Suzanne I. Barchers**

✎ *Super Science: Reader's Theatre Scripts and Extended Activities.* **Lisa Blau**

✎ *Scary Readers Theater,* **Suzanne I. Barchers**

Extension Ideas

✎ The plays can be as elaborately staged as you want, with props and settings.

✎ Children can write their own scripts. *Aaron Shepard's RT page* listed in the web resources has pointers on how to go about this task.

✎ Have a Reader's Theater festival inviting parents and community members. Make sure the children practice before other groups in your program to work out the kinks in the performance.

✎ Form a Reader's Theater troupe as a part of your program offerings. The troupe could work throughout the year and perform for otherafter-school programs, nursing homes, and pre-schools.

"Content Standards"
Reading
Comprehension
✎ Use appropriate strategies when reading for different purposes.
✎ Students read and respond to a wide variety of significant works of children's literature.
Speaking Applications
✎ Engage the audience with appropriate verbal cues, facial expressions and gestures.

** Check out the websites listed at the end of the book for many different useful websites including those with downloadable scripts.

Riddle Books

Staff Role and Space

Staff should provide examples, lead initial discussion, and provide support and supervision.

Can be done in any space, but best if participants can work at tables.

Time

Prep Time: Time to gather materials
Minimum time needed:
   Two 45-minute sessions

Supplies

Cardboard
Masking or strapping tape
Construction paper, writing paper
Paper fasteners/brads (2" recommended)
Crayons, pencils
Coin size manila envelopes 2 1/2" x 3 1/2"
Index cards, cut into 2" x 3" slips
Glue
Scissors

Adaptation/Modifications

✎ To make the books faster, just staple two pieces of construction paper as the covers and writing paper in the middle.
✎ When working with children whose primary language is other than English, find riddles in their languages.
✎ Students can work in pairs, one writing and one illustrating.
✎ Have younger children dictate their riddles and then have them copy the answers to slip in the envelope.

Purpose

To experience the process of book making and to increase reading comprehension.

Directions

Making a Hinged Book:

1. Cut two pieces of cardboard at least 9" by 12".

2. Cover one side of each of the pieces of cardboard with construction paper.

3. Cut a 1" strip off the top of *one* of the pieces of cardboard. This will be used to make the hinge. (Fig. 1)

4. Lay the 1" strip and the rest of the piece of covered cardboard next to each with about a 1/2" gap between the two pieces.

5. Tape the two pieces together using wide packing or masking tape, front and back, making sure that you leave the 1/2" space between the two pieces. (If you do not leave a space the cover will not open.) (Fig. 2)

6. Punch three holes on the inner edge of the front and back cover. Make sure the holes are aligned. (Fig. 3)

7. Place writing paper under the front cover and punch holes in the paper again so they are aligned with the front and back cover. (Use as many pieces of paper as you want pages in your book.)

8. Put the front, back and writing paper together by inserting and closing a paper fastener through each hole.

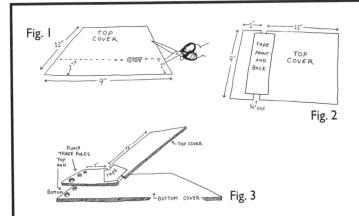

Fig. 1

Fig. 2

Fig. 3

Writing the Book:

1. Have the children read riddle and joke books and find their favorites.

2. On the first page of the book, have the children write their book title, their own name as author and illustrator, and date of publication.

3. For each question or riddle they are going to use, there should be facing pages, the left side for the question and the right side for the answer envelope.

4. Glue the envelope on the right side of the page with the flap facing out.

5. Have the children write their riddles on the left side large enough to fill the page. Work with them to assure proper spelling and punctuation.

6. Encourage the children to make up their own riddles.

7. Have them write the answer on the 2" x 3" card and slip it into the envelope.

8. Decorate the pages, and the cover of the book.

9. Exchange books and have the children try to answer each other's riddles.

Riddle Books

✎ *Biggest Riddle Book in the World,* **Joseph Rosenbloom**

✎ *Best Riddle Book Ever,* **Charles Keller**
Science:

✎ *Starry Skies: Questions, Facts and Riddles About the Universe,* **Mike Artell**

✎ *The Brain Explorer:* **Exploratorium Staff**

Extension Ideas

✎ Write question and answer books on other topics such as weather, animals, and countries.

✎ Have older children take their riddle books and share them with younger children.

✎ The Hinged Book format can be used for the publication of any kind of writing. The children can write and illustrate poetry or short stories and publish them in hinged books.

✎ Visit a publishing company or go to a business that has a printing department to see how books or reports are made.

"Content Standards"
Reading
Word Recognition
✎ Read narrative and expository text aloud.
Writing Strategies
Penmanship
✎ Write fluidly and legibly in cursive.
Written and Oral English Language Conventions
✎ Students write with a command of standard English conventions.

** Check out the websites listed at the end of the book for great links to different riddles and jokes.

9 to 10

9-10 year olds
Transitional - Independent Readers
Younger and older children will also enjoy!

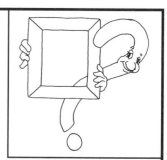

Secret Messages

Staff Role and Space

Staff should give initial directions and provide support and supervision.
Can be done in any space, but best if participants can work at tables.

Time

Prep Time: Time to gather materials
Minimum time needed:
At least 45 minutes, or two days if you want to give the secret messages time to dry completely. Frames can be decorated while ink dries.

Supplies

Invisible Inks:
- Lemon or grapefruit juice
- Milk
- Vinegar

Cotton swabs or small paint brushes
Small cups
Lamp with light bulb
Construction paper, White paper (**Make sure the paper you use is NOT *acid-free* paper.** Many papers used for computer and copying are acid free.)
Scissors
Glue
Decorating materials: crayons, glitter

Adaptation/Modifications

✎ Children who can not write yet can dictate a message to a staff member, then copy the words that the staff member has written.
✎ Children can draw a picture or write one alphabet letter and illustrate their message. Do the same with sight words.
✎ Older children can write more sophisticated messages.

Purpose

To practice writing letters and words and reading them.

Directions

1. Make a frame for the secret message:
   a. Fold a piece of construction paper in half.
   b. Cut a square in the construction paper starting from the folded edge. When you open the construction paper, there should be a square in the middle. (Fig. 1)
2. Glue a piece of white paper onto the construction paper allowing for a blank white area in the middle of the frame for children to write in. (Fig. 2)
3. Dip the cotton swab into the lemon juice, milk or vinegar. Use the cotton swab tip like a pencil and write a message on the paper. (Fig. 3)
4. Let the words dry completely. They should be invisible. *This can take a long time, so make sure the children have something to do while they are waiting.*
5. Decorate the frame.

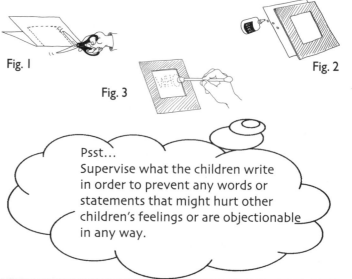

Fig. 1

Fig. 2

Fig. 3

Psst...
Supervise what the children write in order to prevent any words or statements that might hurt other children's feelings or are objectionable in any way.

6. Exchange message frames with other children.

7. Place the paper carefully near a light bulb that is on. *Make sure the paper does not directly touch the light bulb.* The message should reappear.

8. If you want the message to reappear faster, place the paper under a brown paper bag and iron the bag. The message will appear.

Try this one: *Use distilled water.*
1. Mix a little bit of starch or white flour in about a teaspoon of water.

2. Use this mixture as "ink" and write a message on a piece of paper.

3. Let the message dry.

4. Add a little bit of iodine to a teaspoon of water. (You can find iodine in any drugstore.)

5. With a cotton swab, take the solution of iodine and water and paint over the invisible ink. Blue writing will appear.

Other resources for easy science activities
✎ *Science Art: Projects and Activities that Teach Science Concepts and Develop Process Skills*, **Deborah Schecter**

✎ *Showy Science: Exciting Hand-On Activities that Explore the World Around Us*, **Hy Kim**

✎ *365 Simple Science Experiments With Everyday Materials*, **Richard Churchill et al**

✎ *The Science Explorer: Out and About*, **Pat Murphy et al**

Extension Ideas
✎ Make the invisible writing activity part of a "Mystery" unit that will include treasure hunts.

✎ Have a science teacher or someone in the community who knows science come in and example the scientific principles behind the "disappearing ink."

✎ Have the children make greeting cards with invisible messages to send home to family members.

✎ Read "Harry Potter and the Chamber of Secrets" or see the movie, and discuss the role of the diary that was written in invisible ink.

✎ Have the participants carry out an experiment testing which different types of paper result in the best secret messages.

"Content Standards"
Reading
Decoding and Word Recognition
✎ Match all consonant and short vowel sounds to appropriate words.
Writing and Oral English Language Convention
Sentence Structure
✎ Understand and be able to use complete and declarative, interrogative, imperative and exclamatory sentences in writing.

9 to 10

Taste Test Relays

Staff Role and Space

The staff will set up the game area, provide explanation of game and supervise children. One adult needs to be situated at the finish line, and one at the table.

An open space that allows for running and cheering is required. A group of 6-12 children is best for this activity.

Time

Prep Time: Time to gather materials and prepare direction cards
Minimum time needed:
  45-minute session

Supplies

A bag of sour hard candies in a variety of flavors. Jolly Ranchers® are a favorite
Table or box to set supplies on
Two blindfolds or scarves
Two plastic bowls
Pencils and scrap paper
A whistle or bell to signal "go"
Cones or markers

Adaptation/Modifications

✎ You may have the relay area short to accommodate children who are unable to run back and forth.
✎ The adult at the table may help the children with writing, but do not worry about the spelling.

Purpose

For children to learn the concept and the relationship between taste and smell, and practice following written directions and taking dictation.

Directions

This is a traditional team relay race game. See relay race directions below.

Taste Test Explanation

Have a table set up at the finish line with:
✎ Two bowls filled with a variety of flavored hard candies
✎ Two blindfolds
✎ Two cards with the taste test directions written on them
✎ Two pads of paper and two pencils

1. Divide the group into two teams.

2. Each team will send a pair of children to the table. One child puts on a blindfold and plugs his or her nose.

3. After the blindfold is in place, the other child reads aloud the directions on the card:

Directions on Card:
1. I am going to pick up two candies of the same flavor.
2. I will unwrap them and give you one, and I will keep one.
3. With your nose plugged and the blindfold on, guess the flavor.
4. I will write down your guesses.
5. If you make two wrong guesses, unplug your nose and try again.

4. Have the children follow the directions. Make sure the child writes down the other's guesses.

5. The staff member has to be sure that the children read the directions and write the guesses down. If they fail to read or follow the order exactly, they have to begin again.

6. After all directions are followed exactly and a correct guess given, the child takes off the blindfold and the pair races back to the starting line to tag the next pair.

7. After all the pairs guess correctly, the game is over.

Traditional Relay Race Rules

Gather the children and explain the rules of the game:

a. This is a relay game. We will have two teams competing to complete the activity. We will all be winners because we all will learn, have fun and enjoy a special treat.

b. Each team will line up behind the cones. When the whistle is blown, we begin.

c. Two children from each team will run to the finish line and follow the directions on the card. When they are done, and correct, they run back and tag the next two team members to go.

d. The first team to have all of its members successfully complete the task and return to the starting line wins!

Post Game Discussion Prompts

✎ Were you able to guess the flavor of the candy?

✎ Was it easier to guess when you unplugged your nose?

✎ Why?

✎ What were some of the guesses written down which were wrong?

✎ What about the children without the blindfold on and their noses plugged? Was it hard for you to believe your partner was unable to guess correctly?

✎ Are there any patterns of mistakes?

Extension Ideas

✎ Write a five sense poem about the candy:

Line 1—Smell
Line 2—Taste
Line 3—Look
Line 4—Feel
Line 5—Hear

✎ Omit the race and add this to your science activity area with children recording the data in their science journals.

✎ Plan a visit to a local university's science department.

✎ Have local science university student visit your program and share other simple science activities.

✎ Try this exercise with other foods like ice cream. Choose foods that have the same texture, but different flavors such as yogurt.

"Content Standards"

Reading
Comprehension
✎ Follow multiple step instructions.
Listening And Speaking Strategies
Comprehension
✎ Give precise directions and instructions.
Delivery of oral communication
✎ Emphasize points that help the listener follow important ideas and concepts.

Tissue Paper Stories

Staff Role and Space

Staff should give initial directions, provide support and supervision.
Can be done in any space, but best if participants can work at tables.

Time

Prep Time: Time to gather materials
Minimum time needed:
For quality stories allow for two 45 minute sessions.

Supplies

White paper
Different colored tissue paper
12" x 18" White construction paper
Rubber cement - (Glue sticks tend to rip the tissue paper and bottled glue causes wrinkles)
Lined paper cut into 6 x 8 pieces
Scissors
Pens or pencils

Adaptation/Modifications

✎ Children can work in groups or individually.
✎ If you want to display the projects, have the children write rough drafts of the stories that they are going to attach. Correct for spelling and grammar and have them re-write before gluing the paper to the construction paper.

Purpose

To learn about how illustrations support the enjoyment of stories.

Directions

1. Read one of the books by Eric Carle or Marguerite Davol to the children and talk about how the author illustrated them with tissue paper collages.

2. Brainstorm different storylines that they might want to write about. Make a list of ideas and allow the children to choose one. (Let the children either start with the story or start with the illustration, depending on their own style of working, just change the order of directions.)

3. Turn a 12" x 18" construction paper so that the bottom of the sheet is the 12" side. Make a 6" fold in the paper, so that the drawing area is 12" x 12". Tell the children to use that area only for their illustration because the story will be glued underneath it. (Fig. 1)

4. Have them draw an outline of a picture that will be used to illustrate the story on the 12" x 12" area of the construction paper. Talk about leaving space in their outlines that will be filled with the tissue paper. (Fig. 2)

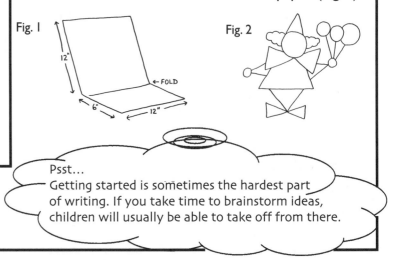

Fig. 1 12" ← FOLD 6" 12"

Fig. 2

Psst...
Getting started is sometimes the hardest part of writing. If you take time to brainstorm ideas, children will usually be able to take off from there.

5. Have the children decide what color of tissue paper they are going to use. Have them begin to cut out the shapes to fill their outlines. Encourage them not to cut out the exact shapes of their outline so that they can have more interesting patterns as they overlap the tissue paper to fill the area.

6. Have children lay out the tissue shapes onto the picture. Tell them to make any changes they want now.

7. Begin gluing down the pieces after they are where the children want them to be. Have the children stop occasionally to look at what they are doing to make sure they make any changes they want. Encourage them to add colors and other shapes to illustrate the story they are going to write. (Fig. 3)

8. Have them write the story that goes along with their illustration on the lined paper. Make sure they have a title. If they want to make a longer story they can glue a page underneath or make another illustrated page.

9. Have children glue the story under the line on the construction paper. (Fig. 4)

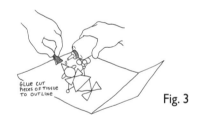
GLUE CUT PIECES OF TISSUE TO OUTLINE

Fig. 3

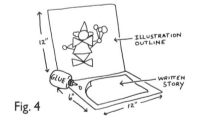
12"
ILLUSTRATION OUTLINE
GLUE
WRITTEN STORY
6"
12"

Fig. 4

** Check out the website lists at the end of the book for a link to Family Crafts: Printmaking

Extension Ideas
✎ Have the children illustrate an entire story.
✎ Explore different books that are highly illustrated and discuss how the illustrations affect the enjoyment of reading the story.
✎ Try out different kind of print-making strategies such as tissue paper print making, leaf prints etc. (See the website in the resources section.)
✎ Make illustrated books for special occasions like Mother's Day, Christmas, Bar Mitzvahs, etc.
✎ Invite a printmaker to the program to discuss the process he or she uses to make art.

"Content Standards"
Reading
Literary Criticism
✎ Evaluate the author's use of various techniques to influence reader's perspectives.
Writing Applications
✎ Write narratives by showing, rather than telling the events of the story.

Suggested Resources
Picture Books Illustrated with Tissue Paper Collages:
✎ Any book by **Eric Carle**
    Do You Want to be My Friend?
    The Very Busy Spider
    The Grouchy Lady Bug
✎ *The Paper Dragon,* **Marguerite Davol, Robert Sabuda**

Paper Making & Illustration:
✎ *Paper (Craft Workshop, No. 1)* **Helen Bliss, Ruth Thomson**
✎ *You Can Make a Collage: A Very Simple How-To Book,* **Eric Carle**

9 to 10

Treasure Hunt

Staff Role and Space

✎ *This activity takes at least two staff members, one to supervise the children developing the directions, and one supervising children who are working inside.*

✎ *Staff should provide examples and lead initial discussion and provide support and supervision.*

Can be done in any space, but much more fun if done outside.

Time

Prep Time: Time to gather materials. If staff plan to hold a treasure hunt as an initial example, its prep time could take 45 minutes.

Minimum time needed:

Two 45-minute sessions for all groups to be able to both plan and participate in a Treasure Hunt.

Supplies

A "treasure," something that participants will find at the end of the hunt
Paper and pencil
Decorating supplies like crayons, colored pencils, markers
Compass (optional)
Measuring tape (optional)

Adaptation/Modifications

✎ Organize your teams so that you have children who excel in writing, drawing and spatial understanding.

✎ Make sure that all the children are involved in reading the directions, not just the best reader. You can have them take turns reading directions.

Purpose

To provide opportunities for participants to write, read and follow technical directions.

Directions

1. Introduce the idea of a treasure hunt. Ask the children if they know any examples of ones. If you have time, read one of the stories listed in the resources. Make sure they understand that treasure hunt maps include:

> ✎ step-by-step directions on how to get from one point to another point
> ✎ a clear beginning point and a clear ending point

2. Brainstorm different words or phrases the children might use on their hunt directions. (See next page for suggestions.)

3. As a complete group, write easy treasure hunt directions to describe how to get from one point in the room to another.

4. Split the large group into smaller groups with no more than 5 children per group.

5. Have one staff member take one group at a time outside to work on writing down, in rough draft form, the clues they are going to use for the hunt they are developing.

6. While the first group is outside, make sure the other children have something to occupy their time, perhaps a word search about treasures.

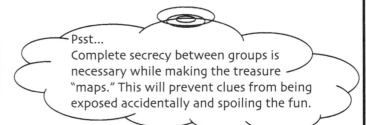

Psst...
Complete secrecy between groups is necessary while making the treasure "maps." This will prevent clues from being exposed accidentally and spoiling the fun.

7. When the first group returns, take out the next group, and repeat until all the groups are finished with their rough drafts.

8. As the groups return, have them develop their hunt directions and create a treasure map. (See the "Bark Paper" activity as a suggestion for making a map.)

9. After everyone is finished, have the groups trade their treasure hunt directions and see if each group can find another group's treasure.

Example of phrases

1. Take _____ giant steps forward *or* backward.
2. Turn to the left *or* Turn to the right.
3. Circle three-fourth way around the _____ going counterclockwise.
4. Take _____ baby steps. (heel to toe)
5. Crawl under *or* over _____.
6. Find the next clue under *or* above _____.
7. Look for a _____ and stand in front of it.
8. Walk straight for _____ yards *or* feet.
9. Face to the right *or* left *or* forward from the _____.
10. Jump three steps forward.

Other action words

pace, jog, slide, hop, jump, crawl, tip-toe, crab-walk— moving with both hands and feet on the ground, with the back toward the ground, face up.

Suggested Resources
✎ *Treasure Hunts! Treasure Hunts* by **Lenny Hort**. Great and inexpensive resource with a lot of ideas for putting on different types of treasure hunts.

Fiction and non-fiction:
✎ *Encyclopedia Brown and the Case of the Treasure Hunt,* by **Donald J. Sobol**
✎ *True-Life Treasure Hunts,* by **Judy Donnelly**
✎ *The Sapphire Princess Hunts for Treasure (Jewel Kingdom , No 6),* by **Jahnna N. Malcolm**
✎ *The Seven Treasure Hunts,* by **Jennifer Barrett**
✎ *The Mummy: Treasure Hunt* ™, by **Jackie Gaff**

Extension Ideas
✎ There are many variations to organizing treasure hunts. For example, have the children write clues that lead to another clue and so forth until the treasure is found.
✎ Read the book "Treasure Island," by Robert Louis Stevenson to the children, perhaps a chapter a day during quiet time. Or, watch the movie as a special rainy day treat.
✎ Teach the children how to use a compass. Have them develop a treasure map or clue sheet using compass directions.
✎ Put on a scavenger hunt. Have one group of children write up the list for another group.
✎ Invite someone who has a metal detector to come in and show the children how it works. Have them explore the area around the program site.

"Content Standards"
Reading
✎ Follow multiple-step instructions in a basic technical manual.
Writing Applications
Write technical documents:
✎ Identify the sequence of activities needed to design a system.
✎ Include all the factors and variables that need to be considered.
Written and Oral English Language Conventions
✎ Students write and speak with a command of standard English conventions appropriate to the grade level.

Waves of Sound

Staff Role and Space

Staff may set up the science stations before children arrive, or have the children create them. Staff will supervise and prompt discussions. It is suggested that no more than 10 children at a time participate in the activity. For more children, use twice as many cans and set up twice as many science stations.
Tables for each center.

Time

Prep Time: Gathering the materials and setting up the stations including making the signs
Minimum Time Needed:
   45-minute session

Supplies

Science Journals (see Simple Science Journal directions on next page)
Two tin cans
6 foot piece of elastic or a chain of large rubber bands
6 foot piece of string
Both a metal and a plastic Slinky®
Pencils

Adaptation/Modifications

✎ You may post journal criteria for the children to meet. These can include questions or ideas for experiments.
✎ Allow children to write in their home language.
✎ Older children can write descriptions of experiments for other children to follow.
✎ Be open to many questions and different experiments that this activity will encourage.

Purpose

To practice recording observations, predictions and hypotheses in journals through an experiment with sound waves.

Directions

Preparing Materials for Sound Stations

Stations One and Two:
✎ With the cork screw punch a hole in the bottom of two tin cans.

> *Station One:* Thread a string through the hole in one can. Tie a knot on the end of the string to keep it in place.
> *Station Two:* Thread a piece of elastic through the other can. Tie a knot on the end of the elastic to keep it in place.

Stations Three and Four:
✎ Place a metal Slinky at station three and a plastic Slinky at station four. Be aware that these Slinkies will be stretched out of shape.

Prepare colorful, fun signs explaining the directions of the stations and prompt questions for the journals. Place them out for the children to access and enjoy.

Activity Process

1. Discuss with children how sound travels. A few points to share include:
✎ *What happens when you drop a small pebble into a bucket or sink of water? What happens to the water? Notice the waves and explain to the children that sounds make the same type of waves as they travel through the air.*
✎ *When we speak, our vocal chords vibrate. These vibrations travel through the air as waves. When these sound waves reach our ear drums, they then vibrate our ear drums and we hear them.*

2. Have the children pair up with a science buddy. These activities will be done with a partner.

3. Explain to the children that they will be experimenting and recording their predictions and observations. Before they do an experiment, they should write down what they think will happen. This may also be referred to as their hypothesis. After the experiment, they will write down their observation and conclusions.

4. **Station One:** Now, one child will hold the tin can up to their ear and their partner will pull the string or elastic taut and strum, making it twang. Have the child listening, record what they hear. Switch roles so each partner gets a turn listening.

5. **Station Two:** When they use the Slinky, have both partners hold one end up to their ear and then strum the Slinky.

6. Have the children rotate through the different sound stations and compare the sounds.

7. After all the children have had time to explore and record, pull the group together to discuss the process and outcomes.

✎ What did they learn?

✎ What other experiments would they like to try?

✎ Encourage children to ask more questions and explain what they observed.

Simple Science Journals

(See a sample on p. 59 in Sponge Garden activity)

✎ Using any size **paper** (5" x 7" works great), stack approximately 15 sheets neatly together.

✎ Create two holes with a paper **hole punch** approximately one inch apart at the top of the stack of paper.

✎ From underneath the paper, push a large **rubber band** up through the holes. The ends of the rubber band will be poking out of the holes on the front side of the paper.

✎ Slip a **Popsicle stick** through the top ends of the rubber band to secure the paper.

✎ Children may decorate the cover of their Simple Science Journal.

Psst…
This activity meets many Science Content Standards. Being able to integrate curriculum is a benefit of quality after-school programs!

Extension Ideas

✎ Purchase lab coats or goggles from a second hand store or donated from a lab, and let the children wear them when participating in science activities. This adds a lot of fun! Have the children write the requests for the donations and send thank-you cards.

✎ Borrow science activity books from the library and encourage children to choose activities to do as a group.

✎ Host a science fair and invite parents to attend.

✎ Experiment with sound waves and different materials.

✎ Science journals should always be available to the children to add information and reflect on past experiments.

"Content Standards"
Listening and Speaking Strategies
Comprehension
✎ Ask questions to seek information not already discussed.
Writing Application
✎ Write research reports about important ideas.
✎ Frame questions that direct the investigation.
Written Language Conventions
Sentence Structure
✎ Use simple and compound sentences in writing and speaking.

Word Pictures
Concrete Poetry

Staff Role and Space

Staff should provide examples, lead initial discussion, provide support and supervision.

Can be done in any space, but best if participants can work at tables.

Time

Prep Time Needed: Time to gather materials

Minimum time needed:
45-minute session

Supplies

White paper
Scrap paper
Pencils and pens
Thesaurus
Crayons and other material for decorating the papers.

Adaptation/Modifications

✎ Younger children can make a picture poem using just the name of the object or just the first letter.

✎ Children can work individually or in groups.

Purpose

To learn to be playful with language, especially descriptive language.

> **Definition:** Concrete poems are made up of words, phrases and sentences that are arranged to make a picture of the subject of the poem.

Directions

1. Have children look at and listen to different examples of concrete poetry. (See suggested resources.)

2. Brainstorm different objects that they can use as a topic for picture poems.

3. Do one poem together. Choose an object, and have them come up with words to describe it.

> *If they come up with a word, have them look it up in the thesaurus and find all the synonyms. List those also. For instance, if they are describing a leaf they might use the word "falling." Other words they might find in the thesaurus are "floating," "dropping."*

4. Have the children lightly draw an outline of the object with a pencil. You can have them trace objects like leaves.

> Psst...
> Using the thesaurus makes this activity so much richer. Most children love to learn new words and are fascinated and empowered by them.

5. On the scrap paper, have the children write down phrases, individual words and sentences that describe the object. They can write about

- ✎ What it looks like
- ✎ How it feels
- ✎ How it makes them feel
- ✎ What they would do with it

Encourage them to answer these questions in phrases, not sentences.

6. Have them substitute the words, phrases and sentences for the lines of the picture, so the words themselves make the picture.

7. Erase the lines so that the words alone make the picture.

8. Decorate the background of the poem.

Suggested Resources

✎ *Doodle Dandies: Poems that Take Shape,* **J. Patrick Lewis**

✎ *Outside the Lines: Poetry at Play,* **Brad Burg**

✎ *A Poke in the I,* **Paul B. Janeczko**

✎ *Splish, Splash,* **Jane Bransfield Graham**

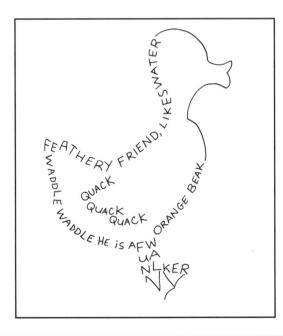

Extension Ideas

✎ Make a poetry book from the participants' poems and donate it to the school or after-school library.

✎ Make the poems the size of the large chart paper and have a "poetry" art show, inviting parents and community members.

✎ Have them "write" their poems on the playground with sidewalk chalk.

✎ Have middle-school age children choose topics that relate to community concerns or more abstract concepts, such as violence, pollution, peace. Have them think of a symbol that will be represented by the words.

"Content Standards"
Reading
Vocabulary and Concept Development
✎ Use a thesaurus to determine related words and concepts.
Writing Strategies
Organization and Focus
✎ Select a focus, an organizational structure.

9 to 10

Write a Rap

Staff Role and Space

Staff provide direction and supervision. Any space is fine!

Time

Prep Time: Time to gather materials
Minimum time needed:
    An initial 30-minute session

Supplies

Pencils
Paper
Thesaurus
Dictionary
Drums or other instruments as desired
Rhyming dictionaries (optional)
    ✎ *Time to Rhyme: A Rhyming Dictionary,*
Marvin Terban
    ✎ *Scholastic Rhyming Dictionary*

Adaptation/Modifications

✎ For children who have a difficult time getting started, prepare an outline of a rap for them.
✎ Allow children to rap in their home language.
✎ Clap the syllables of each word to help beginners.

Purpose

For children to express themselves while writing creatively and learn the connection between poetry, rhyming and rapping.

Directions

1. Share with the children these few facts:

    ✎ Rap stands for rhythm and poetry
    ✎ Rap does not always need to rhyme
    ✎ Rap has a strong rhythm, a strong beat
    ✎ Rap is meant to be shared with others
    ✎ When singing rap, words that rhyme should be louder than the other words.

2. Have the children brainstorm ideas for their own raps. The possibilities are endless.

3. Encourage the use of the thesaurus and dictionary to help expand vocabulary and assist with rhymes.

4. Have the children write their raps and share with each other. This is not a quiet process and many changes may be made before the final rap is complete.

5. As desired, use starter verses, to help the children get started.

6. The children may tap their pencils, drum on drums or clap their hands to get the rhythm.

Psst...
Before sharing popular music with children, be sure to preview the lyrics to ensure they are appropriate for young audiences.

Psst...
Try rapping Dr. Seuss stories!

Starter Verses

She's Cool
She gave us no homework
Because she is cool
She makes it fun to go to school

After School
Bell rings, I'm out the door
With my friends in the yard
I want to dance on the floor
No, it's not hard

Music
The drums go boom, boom, boom
My feet go tap, tap, tap

It's all Good
My friends are here to **stay**
We all meet at three
All we want to do is **play**
Puzzles, video games, **baseball**
It's all good!
Hanging out and **basketball**
There are always people **around**
We never have to be alone
Friends from all over **town**
It's all good!

(Sample Rap by C.M. Glory)

Extension Ideas

✎ Have an evening performance with your Rap Superstars and invite families to join in.
✎ Jump rope along to the raps.
✎ Challenge the children to write raps about specific things they are learning in school.
✎ Visit a local high school to watch their marching band.
✎ Check out poetry books from the local library and try rapping to the various poems.
✎ Create a Rap Star bulletin board with pictures of the children and their rap lyrics written down.
✎ Videotape the children rapping.
✎ Team cheers are also a lot of fun and encourage community spirit!

"Content Standards"
Reading
Literary Response and Analysis
✎ Define how tone or meaning is conveyed in poetry through word choice, figurative language, sentence structure, line length, punctuation, rhythm, repetition, and rhyme.
Listening and Speaking Skills
Organization and Delivery of Oral Communication
✎ Select a focus, organizational structure, and point of view for an oral presentation.
✎ Engage the audience with appropriate verbal cues, facial expressions, and gestures.
Writing
Organization and Focus
✎ Select a focus, an organizational structure, and a point of view based upon purpose, audience, length, and format requirements.

9 to 10

Fun Literacy Activities for After-School Programs

Activities for Children
Ages Eleven Through Fourteen
Independent Readers

1. The activities match the developmental needs of the age of the children because each activity

   - Provides opportunity for more independent planning and increased responsibility,

   - Increases opportunities to impact their community,

   - Increases opportunities to demonstrate their skills to an outside audience,

   - Takes advantage of their increasing interest in the adult world around them, and

   - Provides the participants ways to work in groups to accomplish tasks

2. The activities match the reading, writing and speaking ability of most participants at this age. At this age most participants should be in the following stages of literacy development:

   - **Independent:** They continue to gain greater and greater fluency in reading and writing.

Unit Ideas

   - **Career Exploration Unit:** *Business Cards and Beyond*

   - **Autobiography Unit:** *Time Capsule; I Am Poems; Defending Your Life; Singing the Bios; My Private Thoughts: Journal Writing*

   - **Cooking Unit:** *What's to Eat? Making Cookbooks*

   - **Movie Unit:** *Book Soundtrack*

   - **Cross-Generational Unit:** *Adopt 5th Graders; Defending Your Life; Reading to the Little Guys; Program Director for a Day*

   - **Book Making Unit:** *My Private Thoughts: Journal Writing; Our Book of the Year; Pass It On Books*

Adopt 5th Graders

Staff Role and Space

Staff should lead initial discussion, confirm plans and supervise.

The space necessary will depend on the activities planned by the participants.

Time

This can be scheduled as a long term project, or an ongoing project.

Prep Time: Initially, the staff will have to make arrangements with staff involved with fifth grade groups, and then make copies of action plan forms. Other prep time needed will be defined by the action plan.

Minimum time needed:

One 45-minute planning and prep session

One 45-minute meeting with adoptees

Supplies

A group of 5th graders, or other age group younger than the participants.

Supplies will vary with the chosen activities of the participants.

Adaptation/Modifications

✎ Partner participants in groups that balance talents.

✎ When planning activities with younger participants, consider possible physical limitations and strategies to include everyone.

Purpose

For participants to collaborate as a team and promote positive role modeling for younger children, by 'adopting' 5th graders.

Directions

1. Gather participants together and facilitate a group discussion of community services that involve younger children. Have them brainstorm and record their discussion. Possible discussion leads include:

✎ Were you nervous about starting middle school? If so, what would have helped you be more confident?

✎ What could middle school students do to help out younger 5th grade students?

✎ What are our interests that we could share with younger students?

✎ Where can we find a group of 5th grade students? How do we choose the students who will participate with us?

2. Allow the participants time to organize their brainstorming and outline a plan. Plans should include:

✎ Who are the 5th grade participants
✎ How to invite them
✎ When will they join us
✎ What will we do when they are here
✎ What are our goals for them
✎ How to evaluate our work with them

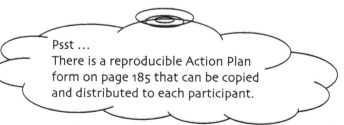

Psst ...
There is a reproducible Action Plan form on page 185 that can be copied and distributed to each participant.

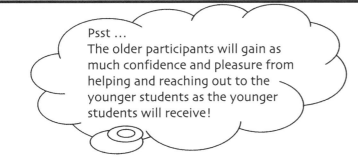

Psst ...
The older participants will gain as much confidence and pleasure from helping and reaching out to the younger students as the younger students will receive!

3. An Action Plan will help organize their goals. See a sample Action Plan in the Yearbook activity on page 144.

4. Have participants invite 5th graders, or other group of younger children, to join them for the various planned activities.

5. Schedule regular meetings for planning and to get together in order to create a long term, or on going, project.

6. Enjoy each other's company!

Activity Ideas

✎ Tutoring and homework support

✎ Reading Club

✎ Music

✎ Dancing

✎ Arts and Crafts

✎ Drama

✎ Science

✎ Community Service

✎ Talent Show

✎ Book Writing

✎ A field trip to a favorite location

✎ Team Survivor (Buddy up younger children with older participants)

✎ Fundraising for a non-profit organization (See *Campaigning for a Good Cause* activity on page 126)

✎ Touring of the Middle School to help younger participants to become familiar with the facilities

Extension Ideas

✎ Invite younger children to help plan a Community Carnival. See activity on page128.

✎ Invite friends and family to visit and enjoy the groups working together!

✎ The older participants can assist the 5th graders in 'adopting' a group of younger children!

✎ The two groups of participants can visit seniors in a nursing home or retirement community.

"Content Standards"

Depending on the activity, all the standards could be integrated into the activity.

Writing Strategies

Research and Technology

✎ Compose documents with appropriate formatting by using word-processing skills and principles of design.

Evaluation and Revision

✎ Revise writing to improve the organization and consistency of ideas within and between paragraphs.

Activities that support Literacy Development

✎ Record brainstorming discussions

✎ Compose Action Plan

✎ Write letters of intent and invitations to younger children

✎ Survey all participants after the activity to determine successes and future plans

✎ Read with younger children

✎ Create Certificates of Participation to 5th graders

✎ Create posters, signs, flyers and schedules of activities such as a show or a get-together

✎ Thank you cards to donors

Reproducible on p. 185

11 to 14

Book Soundtrack

Staff Role and Space

Adult will lead discussion, monitor music selection for appropriateness. Make sure one of the staff is familiar with the music mix process.

Can be done in any space, but best if done in area where the music will not disturb other participants.

Time

Prep Time: Time to gather materials and practice making mixes.

Minimum time needed:
Three 45-minute sessions

Supplies

Variety of books
Recording system: Tape deck with the ability to tape from one tape to another or a CD-Rom Burner
Participant music selections. (You can go to the library and borrow many different kinds of music.)

Adaptation/Modifications

✎ Let the participants choose the books for the activity. They will choose books they can read and enjoy.

✎ Let kids work together in teams. Find out who knows the most about music, most about making "mixes" and who enjoys reading. Put them together so that everyone has a role.

Purpose

To have participants identify mood in stories.

Directions

1. Talk to the participants about their favorite music soundtracks. Discuss how they think the producers of the movie choose the music for the movie.

2. Tell them to pretend they are going to produce the soundtrack for a book that is going to be made into a movie.

3. To get them in the mood have them complete the worksheet "Making a Movie." A replicable worksheet is found on page 180.

4. Put the participants into groups of four. Have them choose a book to read. It can be of any length. Even picture books have enough going on to make a good mix. Short stories also work.

5. As they read, have them make a list of the scenes that need music.

6. Have the group choose the songs for the scenes. Encourage them to experiment with different types of music.

7. Have them "defend" their choices in relation to the mood they are trying to capture with the music.

8. Record a "mix" of the songs.

9. Encourage participants to make an "album" cover for their mix.

Psst...
You're probably going to need to set down some ground rules on what music is acceptable. For example, you might make agreements about not allowing lyrics that glorify violence, gratuitous sex and bad language.

Making a Movie
(reproducible on page 180)

Imagine that you are a screenwriter. Your job is to plan a film version of the book that you have just read. Follow these steps:

1. **Name:** What name will you be giving the movie?

_____

2. **Who would you cast in the roles of the main characters?**

	Main character	Actors
1.	_____	_____
2.	_____	_____
3.	_____	_____
4.	_____	_____

3. **Where would you film your movie?** List some places where you would film the different scenes.

_____

_____

_____

4. **Mood and Atmosphere:** List some sound effects and music for the background of the movie.

_____

_____

_____

_____

Suggested Books

✏ *Hoops,* **Robert Burleigh** (A poem about Basketball)

✏ *Where the Wild Things Are,* **Maurice Sendak**

✏ Any of the **Goosebumps** series

✏ *Revenge of the Snob Squad,* **Julie Ann Peters**

✏ *Sadako and the Thousand Paper Cranes,* **Eleanor Coerr**

✏ *The Gold Cadillac,* **Mildred Taylor**

Extension Ideas

✏ Make this activity part of a movie theme. See the "Story Board" activity on page 60 and "Movie Poster" activity on page 92.

✏ Read the book to an audience with the background music. If your audience is going to be younger kids, then it makes sense to use picture books that are short and quicker to work with.

✏ Watch a video that has a strong soundtrack and have the students discuss how the music affects them.

✏ Visit a sound studio, or have someone who works in one come and talk to your group.

"Content Standards"

Reading

Analysis; Critique/Criticism

✏ Determine mood of various sections of stories.

✏ Students read and respond to literature.

Listening and Speaking

✏ Identify the tone, mood, and emotion conveyed in oral communication.

11 to 14

Reproducible on p. 180

Business Cards & Beyond

Staff Role and Space

Staff will explain process, supervise, collect samples and assist participants.
A comfortable writing area and, if desired, a computer lab area.

Time

Prep Time: An initial discussion and time session is needed to allow children to collect and bring in samples.
Minimum time needed:
   Two or more 45-minute sessions

Supplies

Samples of stationery and business cards. You may request these from parents or neighboring businesses such as the school, a grocery store or offices.
Paper such as card stock (Optional: office supply stores carry business card stock with perforated edges.)
Pens/Pencils
Computer (optional)
Printer (optional)

Adaptation/Modifications

✎ Encourage children to create these items in their home language and for their family members.

Purpose

For children to practice aligning, typing, planning, copying and producing essential business items such as business cards, letterheads and flyers.

Directions

1. Challenge children to collect a large variety of different letterheads, business cards, personalized note pads and similar items. These can be picked up in most businesses, from neighbors, friends, schools, etc.

2. After items are collected, take the time to share and compare. Discussion leads include:

✎ What different styles do we have?

✎ Do different businesses share a common theme or style?

✎ What do you like about the different samples?

✎ What are the company logos and slogans like?

3. Explain to the children that they will be creating their own business products like those collected.

4. Have the children brainstorm and begin planning their layout, designs, colors, slogans and logos. This should be done on scrap paper and allow children as much time as necessary to come up with their ideal format.

5. The final products can either be made free hand, or with the use of a computer. Both methods are acceptable and allow for creativity.

Psst ...
Solicit donations such as card stock, in order to print high quality products.

"No job too small"
**Homework Helper
Marie Perkins**
Call me for patience and assistance with all your homework needs.
Services offered for free after school.

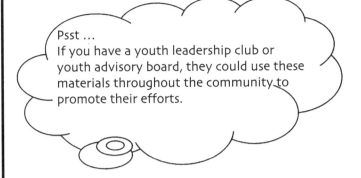

Psst ...
If you have a youth leadership club or youth advisory board, they could use these materials throughout the community to promote their efforts.

Guidelines

✎ Do not allow participants to include personal contact information on their products. If contact information is required, be sure to use your program's general information.

✎ Set up expectations about the type of businesses that are acceptable as themes for their products.

Tips for Creating Cards

✎ Computer programs, such as Publisher and Word, offer templates to make these products.

✎ When formatting with a computer, encourage children to use the tutorials provided by the different computer programs for suggestions, explanations and ideas.

✎ Freehand products offer whimsy and intrigue to viewers.

✎ Artwork, especially children's art, added to products sets them apart from the average.

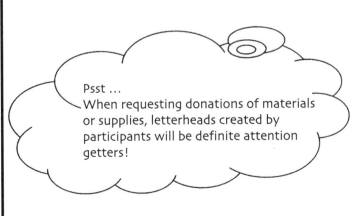

Psst ...
When requesting donations of materials or supplies, letterheads created by participants will be definite attention getters!

Extension Ideas

✎ As a Young Entrepreneur's Club fundraising project, create stationery sets to be personalized.

✎ Have the children offer to create banners, signs, etc. for the different school clubs and associations.

✎ Stationery sets with matching envelopes make great gifts for parents.

✎ Visit a print shop, a stationery store or other local business that sets and copies products.

✎ Mistake items, or extras, can be shared with younger children for the dress up, library or office play centers.

"Content Standards"
Writing Strategies
Organization and Focus

✎ Choose the form of writing that best suits the intended purpose.

✎ Engage the interest of the reader and state a clear purpose.

Research and Technology

✎ Compose documents with appropriate formatting by using word-processing skills and principles of design.

Written and Oral English Language Conventions
Grammar

✎ Identify and properly use indefinite pronouns and present perfect, past perfect, and future perfect verb tenses; ensure that verbs agree with compound subjects.

11 to 14

Campaign for a Good Cause

Staff Role and Space

Staff lead initial discussion and support teams in the development of their ideas. This activity can be done anywhere. It would be best in an area with few distractions and with access to some type of chart paper or board.

Time

Prep time: Time to gather materials
Minimum time needed:
- Selection of the cause: 45 minutes
- Development of the campaign strategy: 45 minutes
- Development of Campaign materials: at least 45 minutes
- Follow through on Campaign: at least two 45-minute sessions
- Debriefing of campaign: 45 minutes
This activity can go on throughout the year.

Supplies

Poster board
Decorating materials: Markers, colored pencils, stencils, magazines for pictures to paste on posters
Writing paper
Computer with word processing program and desktop publishing (optional)

Adaptation/Modifications

✎ Make sure your teams have members with different types of skills including artistic, writing, persuasive speaking.

Purpose

To reinforce persuasive writing and speaking skills, and to provide opportunities for participants to understand the power of language in bringing about change.
Social Action is a very powerful activity for participants of this age. The directions in this activity stress the use of language in social action. Check out the suggested resources for other ways that you can assist your participants in this type of activity.

Directions

1. Brainstorm various issues facing the community or society in general that the participants would like to be able to change. Encourage them to think about issues that they realistically can affect.

2. Have the participants choose one issue they would like to address.

3. Break the larger group into teams of at least four participants. Each team will work on a campaign plan to raise the public's awareness and understanding of the issue.

4. The groups first need to decide on what they want the general public to understand and what they want the public to do. Encourage them to research the issue.

5. The groups will then design the campaign materials including at least
    ✎ a campaign slogan
    ✎ a campaign logo
    ✎ design of posters and/or flyers
    ✎ an editorial
    ✎ information letter

> Psst …
> Support the participants to select an issue that is specific, manageable and directly affects their lives. If they can successfully make a small change they will become empowered to try bigger challenges.

✎ Other materials they can design include a campaign video, a letter-writing campaign, a presentation to the government or school authorities responsible for the area being addressed.

6. Have the smaller groups present their campaigns to the other groups.

7. Decide as a large group what elements of each campaign they want to integrate into their overall campaign.

8. If you plan to carry out the campaign, develop a strategy, deciding on a time line and delegating responsibility for tasks.

9. Begin the campaign and see what happens!

Issue Ideas

✎ Cleaning up an abandoned lot and landscaping it

✎ Decreasing violence in the area

✎ Making a playground for little children

✎ Getting blankets for the homeless

✎ Collecting food for the Food Bank

✎ Protecting an endangered species

Suggested Resources

✎ The local newspaper

✎ *Kids with Courage: True Stories About Young People Making a Difference*, **Barbara Lewis**

✎ *The Kid's Guide to Social Action: How to Solve the Social Problems You Choose—and Turn Creative Thinking into Positive Action*, **Barbara A. Lewis**

✎ *The Kid's Guide to Service Projects: Over 500 Service Ideas for Young People Who Want to Make a Difference*, **Barbara A. Lewis**

Extension Ideas

✎ Invite a community activist to speak to the participants. Have the activist help the participants with their campaign.

✎ Go to the town hall and visit with the mayor.

✎ Have the participants follow through with their campaigns. Make sure they define the goal of their campaigns carefully so they have a chance to see success.

✎ Watch the movie, *The Lorax*, a Dr. Seuss story of a character who is a gentle environmentalist. Discuss how an individual can make a difference. If you have a group of mature participants, you can also watch and discuss the movie, *The Power of One*.

"Content Standards"

Reading

Focus on Informational Materials

✎ Read, analyze, and demonstrate comprehension of informational resources.

✎ Locate information by using a variety of consumer, workplace, and public documents.

Writing application

Write persuasive compositions

✎ State a clear position or perspective in support of a proposition or proposal.

✎ Anticipate and address reader concerns and counterarguments.

Listening and Speaking

✎ Listen and demonstrate comprehension of ideas from oral presentations and discussions.

✎ Prepare and present an effective oral presentation.

11 to 14

Carnival Community Project

Staff Role and Space

Staff will provide enthusiasm, support and supervision.

When planning, table space is needed. When creating props and stations, a large messy work area such as a playground or multi-purpose room.

For the event, a field or large playground area.

Time

Prep Time: No initial prep, but participants will need support with material collection throughout the activity

Minimum time needed:

This is a long term project
— Five 45-minute planning and prep sessions
— 3 hours for actual event
— Set-up and clean-up time

Supplies

Chart paper or black board
Poster boards
Colored paper
Large cardboard boxes - get these at appliance stores.

Adaptation/Modifications

✎ Have each participant utilize their particular strengths and interests with this activity.

✎ Encourage participants to ask for help from other participants to build team spirit.

Purpose

For participants to plan, organize and host a carnival for younger children.

Literacy activities are embedded throughout this activity.

Directions

1. Discuss with participants the prospect of hosting a carnival for younger children. Explain that they will be making the booths, posters and everything else needed.

2. Provide them with materials to write down their ideas as they brainstorm plans. Some items to discuss include:

✎ The booths (see samples on next page)

✎ Who to invite

✎ Will this be a fundraiser? If so, for what cause and how much will things cost?

✎ Where will it be held?

✎ What committees will we need?

✎ Will guests get prizes? If so, what will they be and where do we get them?

3. Have participants divide into committees. Each committee should plan their roles and tasks.

4. As a large group, with all the committees providing input, create an action plan. Use the action planning form located page 185. See the action plan for *Our Book of the Year* activity on page 144 as an example.

Psst ...
Though a lot of work, the process and outcome of this activity is well worth it. Be aware that this often turns into a favorite annual event!

> Psst ...
> Have participants interview younger children for game ideas to have at the carnival.

5. Schedule regular meeting times for each committee to report their progress and work on their projects.

6. Keep it fun and enjoy the process!

Things to Remember

✎ Create flyers to post and hand out inviting people to the carnival. Be sure to include the basics: who, what, where, when and cost.

✎ Make special hand made invitations for younger children you want to include.

✎ Write proper requests for donations of materials and supplies to local businesses. Follow up with personalized thank you cards.

✎ At each game, post directions on how to play and directions for the people working the booths. Be specific!

✎ On the day of the event, be sure to post brightly colored signs in the local area with directions to the Carnival.

✎ After the event, have all participants evaluate their work and write down what changes they might make next year.

Booth Ideas

✎ Snack Bar or Bake Sale
✎ Hoola Hoop Contests
✎ Cake, or cupcake, Walk
✎ Bean Bag Toss
✎ Football Throw
✎ Cookie Decorating Booth
✎ Sidewalk Chalk Art Center
✎ Create a Goodie Bag (to put prizes in)
✎ Jewelry Making Booth (use colored macaroni, etc. for small children to string)
✎ Fishing Booth (Guests toss a rope over the fishing wall with a clip attached and they 'catch' a prize.)
✎ Tic-Tac-Toe (Guests attempt to toss three small Nerf balls into muffin tins, three in a row wins.)
✎ Obstacle Course (Use large appliance boxes for guests to crawl through.)

✎ Face Painting
✎ Freeze Dance
✎ Be a Clown!
✎ Water Balloon Toss
✎ A Story Teller Center

Extension Ideas

✎ Invite a local clown, or other children's entertainer, to visit and participate.

✎ Turn this into a Penny Carnival as a fundraising event.

✎ Invite parents and siblings to participate in the planning and the day of the event.

✎ Search for games, decorations and planning ideas online.

✎ Team up with another community organization, such as a senior home, as a partnership for this activity.

✎ Invite the local school band to provide entertainment.

"Content Standards"

Writing Strategies

Organization and Focus

✎ Choose the form of writing (e.g., personal letter, letter to the editor, review, poem, report, narrative) that best suits the intended purpose.

Research and Technology

✎ Use organizational features of electronic text (e.g., bulletin boards, databases, keyword searches, e-mail addresses) to locate information.

✎ Compose documents with appropriate formatting by using word-processing skills and principles of design (e.g., margins, tabs, spacing, columns, page orientation).

11
to
14

Reproducible on p. 185

Coded Messages

Staff Role and Space

Staff should provide examples and lead initial discussion and provide support and supervision.
Can be done in any space.

Time

Prep Time: Time to gather materials and copy handout
Minimum time needed:
   45 minute session

Supplies

Paper
Pencil
Materials to decorate message pages: colored pencils, pens, stencils (optional)

Adaptation/Modifications

✎ Have the participants write their sentences out in regular language. Have someone check to make sure that they have spelled the words correctly. There is nothing so frustrating as trying to break a code when the words are misspelled!

Psst...
Set out ground rules about the content of messages making sure that they are not hurtful or obscene. Have the group decide together about consequences if such messages are written.

Purpose

To practice decoding skills in a fun way.

Directions

1. Introduce the ideas of coded messages to participants. Ask why they think codes were invented.

2. (Optional) Read a story involving codes. Check out the resource list for possibilities.

3. Introduce a method of coding. Use the ideas listed below. Handouts of different codes are available in the appendix.

4. Have the participants try out different codes, by writing messages to each other.

5. Have them write a message in code on a sheet of white paper and then decorate it with images that illustrate the theme about what they wrote.

Examples of Codes

Number Substitutions:

1	2	3	4	5	6	7	8	9	10	11	12	13
a	b	c	d	e	f	g	h	i	j	k	l	m

14	15	16	17	18	19	20	21	22	23	24	25	26
n	o	p	q	r	s	t	u	v	w	x	y	z

You can change the order of the numbers and letter match so that maybe a = 4, r= 1 etc. to make the code harder to break.

You can do the same thing with letter substitutions.
For example: s y m b o l a c e d f g h i j z x w v q r t u p n k
                a b c d e f g h i j k l m n o p q r s t u v w x y z

The Polybius Square

Each letter can be referred to as a pair of numbers: 1,4 is a D. / is used to indicate an end to a word. For example, 2,3, 1,5, 3,2, 3,2, 3,5/ means "Hello." To make the code more complicated you can change the order of the letters, as long as both you and the person who gets the code has a key.

	1	2	3	4	5
1	A	B	C	D	E
2	F	G	H	I	J
3	K	L	M	N	O
4	P	Q	R	S	T
5	U	V	W	X	Y or Z

Book Codes

Both the writer and the receiver have to have the same book in order to use this code. Make sure the editions of the books are the same.

Numbers are used to show the page of the book and the line on the page which a word is to be found. The first word of the sentence on the page and the line listed is the "message" word. Or you can make it more complex by also listing the number of the position of the word on the line. For example, 10 17 8 would be the word found on page 10, line 7, 8th word on the line.

Morse Code

See the handout of codes on page 186 for the way Morse Code uses dashes and dots to represent letters.

Suggested Resources
✎ *Follow the Drinking Gourd*, **Jeanette Winter** (Story of the code used by escaping slaves.)

✎ *Case of the Mysterious Codes,* **John Warner and Peggy Nicholson**

✎ *The Unbreakable Code*, **Sara Hoagland Hunter** (About the Navajo Code Talkers)

✎ *The Secret Code* , **Dana Meachen Rau, Bari Weissman**

✎ *Radio Rescue,* **Lynne Barasch**

Extension Ideas

✎ Provide Cryptograms as an activity for children to work on when they finish homework. Check out the *Discovery School Puzzlemaker* website listed in the back of the book.

✎ Have the children investigate the role of the Navajo Code Talkers during World War II. There is a video called *Navajo Code Talkers: An Epic Story* that might interest older children.

✎ Watch the video *Look What I Found: Making Codes and Solving Mysteries*. It is for ages 5-12, but for middle school, you can use it to have them plan activities for younger children. See Adopt 5th Graders activity on page 120.

✎ Investigate the history of codes through the centuries, including how they were used in war.

✎ Have the participants develop their own codes.

"Content Standards"
Reading
Decoding:
✎ Decode complex word families and regular multi-syllabic words.
Writing
✎ Use complete and correct declarative, interrogative imperative, and exclamatory sentences.

Activity Resources:
✎ *Spy Science : 40 Secret-Sleuthing, Code-Cracking, Spy-Catching Activities for Kids*, **Jim Wiese**

✎ *Codes, Ciphers and Secret Writing*, **Martin Gardner**

✎ *The Secret Code Book*, **Helen Huckle**

Reproducible on p. 186

Crosswords & Word Searches

Staff Role and Space

Staff should provide examples and lead initial discussion of activity.
Crosswords and Word Search Puzzles can be done anywhere.

Time

Prep Time: Gathering of materials
Minimum time:
Two 45-minute sessions

Supplies

Graph paper
Pencils with erasers
Dictionary
Thesaurus
Sample Crosswords and Word Searches
Computer with internet service (optional)
Printer (optional)
Clipboards (optional)

Adaptation/Modifications

✎ Encourage participants to create puzzles in their home language.
✎ Pair up participants to support and aid each other as needed.

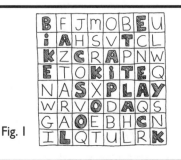

Fig. I

Purpose

For participants to create, and solve, crossword puzzles and word searches while encouraging organization and concept development.

Directions

1. Introduce participants to sample Crosswords and Word Search puzzles. As time allows, have participants enjoy and complete the various sample puzzles.

2. Explain to the participants that they will be making Crossword puzzles and Word Searches. Share with them that:

✎ They will be able to use words and phrases of their own choice in the puzzles.

✎ Both types of puzzles are easier and more fun to create if there is a theme or a specific topic.

Crosswords

1. Brainstorm clues and answers

2. Practice laying out answers on graph paper, connecting the answers to one another with shared letters.

3. Format final puzzle design on graph paper and write clues under the layout. (See example on next page.)

Word Searches

1. Brainstorm words that will be included in the word search.

2. Decide on the size of the word search. Count out the number of squares on the graph paper and mark the boundaries by drawing around the squares.

3. Within the drawing, write the words with one letter per square. Write them left to right, up and down or horizontally.

4. Fill in the extra squares within the drawn square with random letters. (Fig. I)

Music Crossword   by Trenton

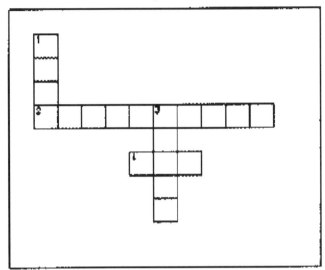

Clues:

Across:
2. Sing here
4. Cool horn

Down:
1. The beat
3. The keys

Drew's Word Search

```
C I S U M S
S G Z X C Y
I Y F H X A
A L O O A L
G O I T R P
L T K E O B
```

Find these words:
1. music
2. play
3. school
4. toys

** See the list of websites at the end of the book for puzzle resources.

Psst ...
Some participants may enjoy making the puzzles, while others prefer to solve them. Either way, they are building skills and having fun!

Answers to Trenton's Puzzle
1. Drum
2. Microphone
3. Piano
4. Sax

Extension Ideas
✎ Try creating personalized mazes!
✎ Have a crossword, or word search, tournament!
✎ Older children can create personalized puzzles for the younger children.
✎ Challenge participants to complete the crossword puzzles found in magazines or newspapers.
✎ Create crossword books which include a puzzle from each participant!

"Content Standards"
Reading
Decoding and Word Recognition
(Reinforces all the decoding skills)
Vocabulary and Concept Development
✎ Clarify word meanings through the use of definition, example, restatement, or contrast.
Writing
Organization and Focus
✎ Create an organizational structure that balances all aspects of the composition and uses effective transitions between sentences to unify important ideas.
✎ Support all statements and claims with anecdotes, descriptions, facts and statistics, and specific examples.
Research and Technology
✎ Create documents by using word-processing skills and publishing programs.

11 to 14

Defending Your Life

Staff Role and Space

Staff should lead initial discussion and then support teams in the development of their ideas.

This activity can be done anywhere. It would be best in an area with few distractions and with access to some type of chart paper or board.

Time

Prep Time: Time to gather materials and make copies of outline

Minimum time needed:
Two 45-minute sessions

Supplies

Paper and pencil
Chart paper or board
Speaker's dais or podium (optional)
Poster Board and presentation material (optional)

Adaptation/Modifications

✎ Match participants who can write better with those that have more difficulty.

Purpose

To write a speech to convince older people that teenagers are great.

Directions

1. Have the participants talk about what they think a sixty-year old woman thinks about today's teenagers. You might have them think of someone they know like their grandmother, neighbor or a person at church.

2. Ask them think about both positive and negative things that this person might think. Tell them not to judge whether they agree with these ideas but just to list them. These things might include:

Music	The way teens talk
Clothes	How teens behave

3. Write their ideas down.

4. Talk about how they should talk to an older person to convince them of something.

✎ *What would really turn off an older person if you were talking to them?*
✎ *What kind of words would you have to use?*
✎ *What is important to older people?*

5. As a group, develop arguments that would help change an older person's negative ideas about teenagers.

6. In pairs, have participants come up with a three minute speech convincing an older person that teenagers are good people. Show them that by not writing full sentences in their outline they will be freer when they give the speech to add ideas. Reproducible handout on page 187.

7. Have them give their speeches. Do not try to have more than three speeches in a row. People stop listening after that. You can have different groups give their speeches on different days.

Psst ...
This topic can get the kids angry if not carefully treated. Make sure you have strong expectations on how they should talk and act while doing this activity.

Speech Outline

(Encourage the participants to only write phrases for speech, so they are not tempted to "read" their speech)

Introduction: (for example: personal story, poem, quote)

Main Idea: (What the three main ideas are that you plan to present)

1st idea: Older people may think _____, but it is not true because _____
    example:
    example:
Ending statement:

2nd idea: Older people also may think _____, but it is not true because _____
    example:
    example:
Ending statement:

3rd idea: Older people may also think _____, but it is not true because_____
    example:
    example:
Ending statement:

Conclusion: (What older people and teenagers can do to appreciate each other is one possibility.)

Extension Ideas

✎ Invite older people in the community to spend some time talking to the participants.

✎ Have a competition to identify the best speech. Invite a local person of importance to judge the speeches.

✎ Arrange for the participants to go and give their talks to local civic organizations.

✎ Include this activity in a cross-generational theme.

✎ If you are working with computers, have them develop a Power Point presentation.

"Content Standards"
Listening and Speaking

✎ Determine the speaker's attitude toward the subject.

✎ Select a focus, an organizational structure, and a point of view, matching the purpose, message, occasion, and vocal modulation to the audience.

11
to
14

Reproducible on p. 187

I Am...

Staff Role and Space

Staff lead initial discussion and then support individuals in the development of their ideas. Make sure the participants know what nouns are before they begin. This activity can be done anywhere.

Time

Prep Time: Make copies of poem format

Minimum time needed:

45 minutes so re-writing can be supported.

Supplies

Lined paper for drafts
Unlined white paper for final copy
Construction paper (optional)
Decorating materials — colored pencils, markers, glitter (optional)
Stencils (optional)

Adaptation/Modifications

✎ Allow participants to write in their home language.

✎ If necessary, participants can dictate their poems and then re-write them.

✎ Allow for small groups to work together and exchange ideas.

✎ Have participants make rough drafts, and have staff edit.

Purpose

To learn to use words to communicate feelings and to practice writing descriptive poetry.

Directions

1. Brainstorm different things that make each of us unique: things we like and dislike; our physical characteristics; who we are in relation to others; things we can do. Do this brainstorming as a large group, or small groups or even pairs. Make sure you have the groups report on their ideas.

2. Do a large group "We are .... poem" explaining the different parts of the format.

3. Have every person then write their own poems about themselves.

4. Work with them on spelling and getting the right format.

(The following steps are optional but encourage the participants to take better care in the presentation of their poems.)

5. After the participants have written the poems and all corrections have been made, have them re-write them on a clean unlined white paper with black ink pens.

6. Paste the white paper on a piece of construction paper and have them decorate the paper. Make sure they sign them.

Psst ...
If you want the participants to write more complex and interesting poems, the pre-discussion is a critical step. Get them talking before they start writing.

"I Am..." Poem Format

(Reproducible on page 188)

#1. I am

#2. Nouns about which you have strong feelings. Each word starts with a capital letter.

#3. Write a complete sentence about two things that you like.

#4. Nouns that describe what you like to see in other people; end with "are important to me." Capitalize each noun.

#5. Write a sentence containing a positive thought or feeling. It can tell something that you find acceptable in yourself.

#6.-#7. Write sentences in which you show something negative in yourself or others, however the sentence must be showing that out of something BAD can come GOOD. Use the word "but" to link the bad and good.

#8.-#9.-#10. Short sentences relating something about which you have strong feelings—likes or dislikes. They do not have to relate to each other or to the previous lines you have written.

#11. End with "This is me" or "I am."

Sample poem *(by Danielle Green)*:

> I am
>
> Daughter, Friend, Free
> I love reading a good book and listening to music.
> Honesty, Senses of Humor, Craziness are important to me.
> Times to be quiet are necessary for my happiness.
> When people are mean to each other, I want to get mad, but I try to control myself so I am not mean either.
> I love having fun.
> I hate doing homework.
> I enjoy talking to my friends.
> This is me

Extension Ideas

✎ Have an art exhibit that includes the matted poems. Include a poetry reading as part of the show.

✎ Have a local poet or author visit to add enthusiasm to the participants' efforts.

✎ Make a participant poetry book that includes poems and photographs of each of the participants. Look at the *Riddle Book* activity for a description of a hinged book or the *Cook Book* activity for a sewn book style.

✎ Check out the website in the appendix for other poem formats that the participants can use, including poems related to emotions and actions.

✎ Have the participants use the "Feeling Dictionary" in the appendix to find more terms to describe their feelings.

"Content Standards"
Writing Strategies
Evaluation and Revision
✎ Revise writing to improve organization and word choice after checking the logic of the ideas and the precision of the vocabulary.
Written and Oral English Language Conventions
✎ Students write and speak with a command of standard English conventions appropriate to this grade level.

11 to 14

Reproducible on p. 188

Multicultural Game Tournament

Staff Role and Space

Staff lead initial discussion; lead the participants through learning the games and support teams in developing their ideas. This activity requires enough indoor or outdoor space for groups to learn and practice the games; tables, desks or floor space to make the rule posters; enough room to hold the tournament.

Time

Prep Time: Staff need time to either select the games or the reference material for participants to select games; time to gather supplies for the games.

Minimum time needed:

45-minute session: groups go through the reference material and select games (optional)

45-minute session: individual groups learn and practice games

45-minute session: individual groups develop rule posters and decide how to introduce and teach the games

2-hour session: **Tournament**

Supplies

Depends on the games selected
Poster paper
Markers and materials for decorating rule posters

Purpose

To encourage participants to pay careful attention to the writing and reading of rules and procedures.

In order for this activity to be a literacy activity, you must arrange it so that the participants learn the games by reading the directions, not by demonstrating the games to them.

Directions

1. Divide participants into the number of groups that match the number of games you will play in the tournament. For example, if you plan to play six games, you will need six groups. To determine the size of the group decide the minimum number of players needed to play any of the games. For those games that require only two players, you still can have larger teams, just make sure you have enough game boards for each of the pairs.

2. Give each of the teams the rules for the game. They need to learn to play by following the written rules. If someone in the team already knows the game, encourage that person to be the reader. Staff should not tell or demonstrate how to play, but rather encourage the participants to re-read the directions.

3. Have the teams play the games until they have mastered them.

4. The teams should then write out the rules on a poster using the format described on the handout found on page 189. Have them decorate their posters.

5. Each team will take turns teaching other groups their game. Encourage them to refer to their posters as they explain.

6. After everyone has learned all of the games, hold a program tournament with participants choosing the games they will play for their group, or rotate the team members so that each team member plays at least one round of each game.

Suggested Games

The rules for all these games can be found on the suggested websites found in the Website List at the end of the book or in the books listed below.

Inside:

- ✎ **Kulit K'rang:** Indonesia—Similar to jacks
- ✎ **Dominos:** Chinese–Requires buying sets of Dominos
- ✎ **Chinese Checkers:** Chinese—Requires buying sets of Chinese Checkers
- ✎ **Mancala:** African—You can buy Mancala sets or there are many directions for making sets online
- ✎ **Alquerque:** Spain–You can find directions to make a board in the Multicultural Game books or online
- ✎ **Checkers:** English– Requires buying Checkers sets or participants can make boards
- ✎ **Pacheesi:** India—Requires buying a game board
- ✎ **Chess:** India—Requires buying Chess set
- ✎ **Go:** Chinese– Requires buying or making a simple set with pebbles
- ✎ **Battleship:** United States– Can buy the game, or you can use a grid that you can download.

Outside or Gym:

- ✎ **1, 2, 3 Dragon:** Chinese
- ✎ **Bokwele:** Nigeria
- ✎ **Kameshi Ne Mpuku:** The Luba tribe in the Congo (Played similarly to *Streets and Alleys*)
- ✎ **Roman Ball:** Italian
- ✎ **Net Takraw:** Thailand, Burma, Malaysia, Singapore and the Philippines - Similar to volleyball but you can not use your hands
- ✎ **Alto Ahi!:** Argentina
- ✎ **Wolf! Wolf!:** Egyptian
- ✎ **Pebble Tag:** Greek

Suggested Books about Multicultural Games

- ✎ *Children's Games from Around the World,* **Glen Kirchner**
- ✎ *The Multicultural Game Book,* **Louise Orlando**
- ✎ *Multicultural Games,* **Lorraine Barbarash**

Adaptation/Modifications

- ✎ Participants can either choose their own teams or the staff can divide them to assure different kinds and levels of skills are in the various groups.
- ✎ Let participants who prefer not to play the games become the score keepers and "gophers" for the players.
- ✎ Make sure to include physically challenged participants in any way they feel comfortable.

Extension Ideas

- ✎ This activity can be part of a multicultural theme that includes many other activities.
- ✎ Invite members of the community from other countries to talk about and demonstrate the games they played as children.
- ✎ Have the 11-14 year olds organize and put on a multicultural tournament for younger children acting as coaches, scorekeepers and suppliers of materials.
- ✎ Have the participants make up their own games after being given different supplies. Encourage them to make up rules, practice and modify the game and teach it to other participants.

"Content Standards"

Reading

Reading Comprehension

- ✎ Follow multiple-step instructions in a basic technical manual.
- ✎ Analyze text that is organized in sequential order.

Writing Applications

- ✎ Write technical documents that identify the sequence of activities needed to design a system or operate a tool.

Evaluation

- ✎ Revise writing to improve organization and word choice after checking the logic of the ideas and the precision of the vocabulary.

11 to 14

Reproducible on p. 189

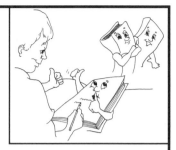

My Private Thoughts: Journal Writing

Staff Role and Space

Staff lead initial discussion and then support individuals to write in their journals by providing time for it during program hours.

Time

Prep time: Gathering of supplies
Minimum time needed:

Making the journal: At least 45 minutes
Journal writing: 15 minutes periodically throughout the program year.

Supplies

Chart paper/ white or chalk board
Book making material: (depends on the type of book you decide to make) See
✎ Hinged books in the *Riddle Book* Activity on page 102.
✎ Books with bindings in the *Cookbook* Activity on page 164.
✎ Simple Construction paper books in *My Own Book* on page 52.
Materials to decorate the covers of the journal: markers, colored pencils/ pens, stencils, magazines for pictures to make collages, scissors, paste

Adaptation/Modifications

✎ Encourage the use of the language the participants are most comfortable with.
✎ Do not edit for grammar or spelling.

Purpose

To encourage participants to creatively express their feelings through writing.

Directions

1. Discuss the reasons why writing is a good way to express feelings. Some reasons you might include are

   ✎ Writing helps clarify our feelings,

   ✎ When we are upset, writing lets us express our emotions without hurting anyone else, and

   ✎ Writing lets us explore our feelings in a much deeper way.

2. Have them make a journal book. Encourage them to take time decorating the cover as an expression of themselves. (See the suggested book making styles listed under Supplies in the box to the left.)

3. On the top of every blank page of the journal, have them write the suggested prompts listed on the next page or brainstorm other ideas. Make sure they write the date of the entry.

4. During the program year, consistently set up a time when the participants write in their journals. When-ever they fill up a journal, have them make another one.

Date: Jan. 20, 2004
One way I am different is that I was adopted from China by my parents.

(Reproducible on page 190)

Prompts to elicit ideas around:

Self –Esteem

One way I am different from everyone else is . . .

Most people think I am . . .

The time when someone made me feel special was . . . .

My parents show me that they like me when . . . . .

I feel encouraged when . . .

I am important because . . .

One thing I do better than anyone else is . . .

Other people are important because . . .

Sense of Autonomy

I think that the teacher's responsibilities are to...

When my mom is upset with me, I . . .

One time, I was afraid to try something new . . .

I tried something that I thought I could do and it . . .

I feel safe asking for help because . . .

Social Skills

When my friend and I disagree about what we want to do, I...

If someone does not like something I do, I would like them to . . .

When I'm upset, I like my friend to . . .

When my mother is angry at me, I would like her to...

If I am afraid of something, I would like my friend to . . .

Decision Making

Something I enjoy doing that others do not is . . .

Once I had a problem that no one else could help me with. I . . .

Some problems I have right now are...

If I could earn my own money, I would feel . . .

The problem I solved on my own was . . . .

Some decisions I made today were . . .

Something about myself (besides my looks) that I would like to change is . . .

Morality and Hope

When I get in trouble, I . . .

The worst thing I ever did to anyone was . . .

One time I did something that I knew I'd get in trouble for, but I did it anyway because . . .

A place that is very special to me is . . .

When I get discouraged, I make myself feel better by . . .

If my friend stole something, I would . . .

When I have to make hard decisions, I . . .

Five of the most important things in my life are . . .

Psst …
Make journal writing an integral part of your program. It is a great way for some participants to get their feelings out in a constructive way.

Extension Ideas

✎ Watch the movie, "The Diary of Anne Frank." Have participants discuss what people will think about their own lives if they read their journal years later.

✎ Have participants write a letter to themselves that they will read in the future. Suggest that they write about their goals for the future, what they see themselves doing in the future, etc. Stress that they should keep the letter safe so they can read it later in their lives.

✎ Develop "program" journals. Have groups of participants make group journals to be used for communication between all group members. These journals can be used as a safe way to bring out concerns. Have some type of ritual for bringing it out everyday and having it available. If there are problems between group members, encourage using the journal to communicate with each other.

"Content Standards"
Writing Applications
Write biographies, autobiographies
✎ Reveal the significance of, or the writer's attitude about, the subject.
Written and Oral English Language Conventions
✎ Students write and speak with a command of standard English conventions appropriate to grade level.

11 to 14

Reproducible on p. 190

Name That Junk

Staff Role and Space

Staff should provide examples and lead initial discussion and then provide support and supervision.

Can be done in any space, but best if participants can work at tables.

Time

Prep Time: Time needed to gather material and make copies of handout

Minimum time needed

At least two 45-minute sessions depending on the complexity of the sculpture

Supplies

Any junk art supplies– Examples: large and small boxes, empty film canisters, paper towel rolls, newspaper, packing peanuts, toothpicks, aluminum foil, plastic bottles

Glue

Prefix/Suffix sheet

Other art supplies: feathers, beads, construction paper, crayons, glitter

Adaptation/Modifications

✎ Participants can work on a sculpture alone or in groups.

✎ If the participants have trouble initially with the idea of forming words, work with them as a whole group with staff leading the activity more directly.

✎ If writing the narrative is difficult have the children dictate their stories to an adult, and then copy the dictated stories.

Purpose

To learn the meaning of common root words, prefixes and suffixes, and understand plot techniques in order to write narratives.

Directions

1. Bring an example of a TRANSFORMER toy and show it to the children. (If you can not get an example, ask the children if they know about them.)

2. Ask them if they can guess how the toy got its name. Explain to them how each part of the name has a meaning that when put together explains the way the toy works.

          <trans> = across, over

        <form> = make

          <er> = a person, thing performing an act

3. Explain to them that they are going to

   ✎ make a sculpture,

   ✎ give it a name using common root words, prefixes and suffixes, and

   ✎ write a story about it.

4. Divide the group into teams of three or four. Provide each group with enough "junk" to make a sculpture.

5. Sit back and let them create.

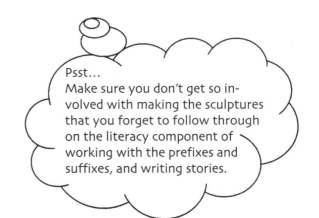

Psst...
Make sure you don't get so involved with making the sculptures that you forget to follow through on the literacy component of working with the prefixes and suffixes, and writing stories.

6. After participants have created their sculptures, have them talk about a name for their object using the root words, prefixes and suffixes on the list found on page 191.

7. Have them try out different combinations and see what meanings they come up with.

8. After they have a name, have them write a story or a poem. Their sculpture should be the character, setting or other main object depending on what form the sculpture takes.

9. Display the sculptures and writings.

Examples of Sculpture Names

SEMI-ASTRORIUM:
Room made up of half a star

SUPER-PAPERTOMY:
Above normal paper cutter

TRANS-GEOSCOPE:
Machine that can look across the world

ULTRA-DENTENT:
Someone who has many teeth

Suggested Resources

✎ *The Art and Craft of Paper Sculpture: A Step-By-Step Guide to Creating 20 Outstanding and Original Paper Projects,* **Paul Jackson**

✎ *Mudworks: Creative Clay, Dough and Modeling Experiences (Bilingual Spanish/English Edition available),* **Mary Ann Kohl**

✎ *Outstanding Art: Imaginative Three Dimensional Art and Sculpture,* **Lilian Coppock**

✎ *Gizmos & Gadgets: Creating Science Contraptions that Work,* **Jill Franklin Hauser.**

Extension Ideas

✎ Put on an art display of the sculptures and the stories, and invite parents and friends.

✎ Work with other sculpting media such as clay and papier mâché. There are great ideas in the suggested resources.

✎ Have the children look through magazines and newspapers for words that have suffixes, prefixes and combining forms. Make it a contest with the team finding the most words in a pre-determined time the winners.

"Content Standards"

Reading:
Vocabulary and Concept Development
✎ Know common roots, suffixes and affixes.
Narrative Analysis
✎ Identify the main events of the plot.

Writing
Writing applications
✎ Write narratives relating ideas, providing a context and using concrete sensory data.

11 to 14

Reproducible on p. 191

Our Book of the Year

Staff Role and Space

Staff will provide initial instruction and support as needed. Staff will need to guide participants because this activity takes a lot of organization and planning. Table tops and computer lab area.

Time

Prep time: Gathering of samples and supplies.

Minimum time needed:

This is a long term project. At least five 45-minute sessions are required. More time will result in a more creative, professional product.

Supplies

Sample yearbooks
Paper
Glue Sticks
Cameras and film
Computer and Printer
Access to a copy machine
Chart paper or chalk board

Adaptation/Modifications

✎ If time is an issue, create newsletters or flyers instead of yearbooks.

✎ Have each participant utilize their particular strengths and interests with this activity.

Psst ...
This is a great summer activity, *Our Summer Yearbook!*

Purpose

For participants to work together as a team to plan, organize, write and publish a collection of memories.

Directions

1. Talk with participants about how they will be working together to create a yearbook.

2. Have participants brainstorm all their ideas about what should be included in a yearbook and the process they will use to write the book. Have them write all these ideas and plans down.

3. Create committees for the various duties. You may consider writers, photographers, editors and lay-out specialists.

4. As a large group, with all the committees providing input, create an action plan. Create on a black board or chart paper. Follow up by writing an action plan using the form found on page 185. You may want to use a format such as this:

Duty	Supplies Needed	Who's Duty	Date Completed	Update	Check In, Report
Plan design	Paper, pens	Design Comm.			✔
Take pictures	Cameras Film $ for processing	Photo Comm. Fundraising Comm.			✔
Write & collect stories	Writing materials, resources	Writers			✔

5. Schedule regular meeting times for each committee to report their progress and work on their projects.

6. Celebrate the publication of the yearbook.

Psst ...
This activity is a wonderful opportunity for parents to volunteer and be involved. They can help keep schedules and deadlines, edit and guide participants.

Things to Consider

✎ Invite all participants at the site to write about their experiences over the year to be included in *Our Book of the Year*.

✎ Provide participants with disposable cameras to take pictures of daily activities and special events.

✎ Include pictures of parents and family members.

✎ Include a memory page with pictures of participants when they were small children.

✎ Include a staff page with pictures and mini-bios of each staff member.

✎ Have a special section for participants who will be graduating this year.

✎ What will be on the front back covers?

✎ Have participants solicit a donation, or reduced price, for printing services.

✎ Charge for local business to advertise in *Our Book of the Year* to raise money for photographs and printing charges.

✎ Keep the yearbook simple and use a copy machine. Bind the books as suggested in one of the following activities:
  ✎ Hinged books, page 102
  ✎ Books with bindings, page 164
  ✎ Simple construction paper books, page 52

✎ Include an autograph section for friends to share well wishes.

✎ Include a "World Beat" section sharing the trends, entertainers and news stories popular during the year.

✎ Have a great time and be creative!

Extension Ideas

✎ If you are located on school grounds, or are associated with a school that does not have an annual yearbook, have the participants offer to help get one started!

✎ Make Season Books, which are similar to yearbooks but are smaller and come out 4 times a year.

✎ Create a student issued newsletter which includes information such as that found in a yearbook.

✎ Have the participants work with younger students to make yearbooks for their programs.

"Content Standards"
Writing Strategies
Organization and Focus
✎ Use a variety of effective and coherent organizational patterns, including comparison and contrast; organization by categories; and arrangement by spatial order, order of importance, or climactic order.
Research and Technology
✎ Compose documents with appropriate formatting by using word-processing skills and principles of design.
Evaluation and Revision
✎ Revise writing to improve the organization and consistency of ideas within and between paragraphs.

11 to 14

Reproducible on p. 185

Pass It On Books

Staff Role and Space

Adults provide direction and supervision.
No particular space requirements!

Time

Prep Time: Time to gather materials.
Minimum time needed:
   45-minute session to get started
   and then open ended.

Supplies

Spiral notebooks or supplies for
children to make their own notebooks
(construction paper, ruled paper,
stapler, etc.)
Pens, pencils

Adaptation/Modification

✎ Buddy up children who may need help
with reading and writing.
✎ Encourage children to use their home
language in these books.

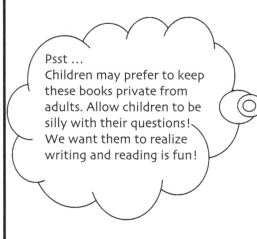

Psst ...
Children may prefer to keep
these books private from
adults. Allow children to be
silly with their questions!
We want them to realize
writing and reading is fun!

Purpose

To have children write questions in notebooks and
have their friends and peers write answers to the
questions directly in the book.

Pass It On Books: *Question and answer books that are
passed around between peers allowing for quick, creative
responses.*

Directions

1. Brainstorm with participants different questions
they might like to ask in an interview of their peers.
Encourage silly questions and questions about popular
trivia, such as favorite TV shows, colors, and movies.
Set clear guidelines about what are acceptable questions and answers to assure that no ones' feelings will
be hurt and that privacy issues are protected.

2. Provide each child with a spiral notebook, or materials to create a note book. Construction paper folded
and stapled to 10-20 sheets of ruled paper usually
works best.

3. Have children decorate and personalize their notebooks.

4. At the top of each sheet of paper in their own book,
the children write a question they would like to ask
the others. Big, bold writing works best. Everyone's
questions will be different, no two books will be alike!

5. After books are all put together, with a question on
each sheet, the children pass their books around and
answer each other's questions. This is typically done
throughout the week. A favorite time to do so is free
time when children can take their time and relax. *Each
child answers every question when they receive a book.*

6. Remind children to sign their names to their answers.

Psst ...
Children get to know a lot about one another through these books!

Pass It On Book Example

from Alla (age 10)

Question: What is your favorite thing to do after school?

"I like to hang out with my friends and eat oranges." C.M.

"Play Volleyball" Z.E.

"Listen to music and talk with my friends." S.N.

Question: Who's your favorite music band?"

"Brittney Spears and Justin Timberlake. I like to dance to their music." A.K.

"Coldplay" S.E.

"I like a lot. No favorite." C.G.

"Name the 7 Dwarfs From Snow White"

"Doc, Sleepy, Grumpy, Dopey and 3 others." L.J.

"What L.J. said, but add Sneezy and 2 more." C.G.

Extension Ideas

✎ Have children compile their answers and create a graph of popular answers.

✎ Create a "Center" *Pass It On Book* to keep in the center.

✎ Create a *Pass It On Book* for parents. Keep it near the sign-in book and encourage parents to participate.

✎ Use some of the questions and answers in a Program Yearbook.

"Content Standards"

Reading

Word Recognition

✎ Read aloud narrative and expository text fluently and accurately and with appropriate pacing, intonation, and expression.

Vocabulary and Concept Development

✎ Identify and interpret figurative language and words with multiple meanings.

Written and Oral English Language Conventions

Sentence Structure

✎ Use simple, compound, and compound-complex sentences; use effective coordination and subordination of ideas to express complete thoughts.

11 to 14

Presto, Magic Show!

Staff Role and Space

Staff will provide magic books, supervision, opportunities and support as needed. Table tops to prepare and clear floor space area to perform.

Time

Prep time: Time to gather materials and schedule practice time as needed.
Minimum time needed:

4 or more 45-minute sessions
- Discussion and plans
- Learn and practice the tricks
- Create posters, invitations and other materials
- **Presto Magic Show!**

Supplies

Books on magic
Poster Board
Markers
Stationery
Large cardboard box (optional)
Magic supplies (optional)

Adaptation/Modifications

✎ Older participants can assist younger children with directions and modification of tricks.
✎ Participants of all abilities can be involved in this activity.

Purpose

For participants to follow directions, practice presentation skills and have fun!

Directions

1. Discuss with participants the idea of learning magic and staging a magic show. Prompt questions may include:

  ✎ Have you ever been to a magic show?
  ✎ Do you know any magic?
  ✎ What type of supplies do magicians use?
  Magic wands and ....
  ✎ How many magic words can we come up with?

2. Supply participants with books on magic and, if possible, watch a video of a magic show.

3. Encourage the participants to plan and present a magic show. This will involve inviting an audience and advertising the event.

4. Make a magician's podium out of a large cardboard box. Paint it bright colors with stars and other magic symbols. (Optional)

Ways to Announce Your Presto Magic Show:
Posters
Invitations
Business Cards
Thank You Cards

Psst ...
For added fun, have the participants create their magician names. For example, Lena Jones may be Lena the Stupendous Magic Superstar!

Presto Tricks to Get You Started

Knot Tie:
Challenge participants to tie a knot in a piece of rope, about 3 feet long, without letting go of the ends. After everyone has a chance to try it, show them how! After all, it is very easy!

✎ When you hand the rope to them, hold the ends with your arms stretched out straight to them.

✎ Tell them to take it, and without letting go of the ends, tie it in a knot.

✎ When they are baffled and hand it back to you, lie it straight on the table.

✎ Criss-cross your arms and pick up the ends of the rope and, without letting go of the ends, uncross your arms and PRESTO MAGIC! You have a knot.

Disappearing Coin:
✎ Sit at a table and show everyone a coin, telling them it will soon disappear.

✎ Dramatically, rub it on your elbow and then act surprised that the trick did not work so announce you will switch hands.

COIN →

✎ Pick the coin up and **pretend** to put it the other hand. Again, rub the coin into your other elbow (just pretend because it is really still in the other hand).

✎ The hand holding the coin will be up near your collar, so drop the coin into your shirt.

✎ Then, TA DA! The coin has disappeared.

✎ Show audience members both hands, no coin!

Extension Ideas
✎ Host a Magic Show for younger children to attend at an elementary school or a preschool.

✎ Presto Magic Show can be combined with a Show of Stars as a fundraising collaboration.

✎ Invite a local magician to teach the children more tricks and presentation skills.

✎ Visit the local library for many magic trick books and videos.

"Content Standards"
Writing Strategies
Organization and Focus

✎ Choose the form of writing that best suits the intended purpose.

✎ Engage the interest of the reader and state a clear purpose.

Listening and Speaking
Organization and Delivery of Oral Communication

✎ Organize information to achieve particular purposes and to appeal to the background and interests of the audience.

✎ Use speaking techniques, including voice modulation, inflection, tempo, enunciation, and eye contact, for effective presentations.

11 to 14

Resources
Books

✎ *Illusions Illustrated: A Professional Magic Show for Young Performers,* **James Baker,**

✎ *Modern Coin Magic,* **J.B Bobo,**

✎ **Easy-To-Do Card Tricks for Children, Karl Fulves**

✎ *A Guide for Using* **The Lion, The Witch and The Wardrobe** *in the Classroom,* **C.S Lewis.**

✎ *Magic for Kids,* **Fay Presto**

✎ *Magic Science: 50 Jaw-Dropping, Mind-Boggling, Head-Scratching Activities for Kids,* **Jim Wiese**

Videos

✎ *Anytime, Anyplace Magic,* **Michael Ammar**

✎ *The Complete Introduction to Coin Magic,* **Michael Ammar**

✎ *Magic's Biggest Secrets Finally Revealed!,* **Val Valentino**

Program Director for the Day

Staff Role and Space

Staff will provide explanations and support as needed. If it is decided that winners will take on a special assignment for a day, staff will need to make prior arrangements with those involved.
Quiet table space works best.

Time

Prep Time: Staff will need to determine the parameters of the responsibilities that the young person will undertake when acting as director.
Minimum time needed:
Two or more 45-minute sessions

Supplies

Black board or flip chart paper for brainstorming
Pencils and pens
Writing paper
Dictionary
Thesaurus
Computer (optional)
Printer (optional)

Adaptation/Modifications

✎ Create teams of participants for support of one another. They can apply for the position as a team!
✎ Staff members can provide an outline of a form letter for participants who may struggle with the process. Such outlines and samples can be found online.

Purpose

For the participants to write a persuasive letter and evaluate the letters of their peers.

Directions

1. Present the participants with the possibility of being the Program Director for the day. Explain to them that there will be a contest for such a title with those interested writing a persuasive letter.

2. Discuss with the participants the intent of a persuasive letter. Someone can write main points of this discussion on the black board or a sheet of flip chart paper. Points to share include:

✎ The purpose of a persuasive letter is to promote something or to change the reader's mind on a matter.

✎ Before writing, consider who your audience is.

✎ What objections and questions might the reader have to your proposal?

✎ Is there a special slant the letter can take to be more persuasive and interesting?

✎ What words and points can be used to assure the reader that the writer is honest, sincere and dedicated?

Psst ...
Acknowledge all participants for their efforts. Perhaps there can be winners such as assistant directors and staff members.

Psst ...
The winner typically 'shadows' the Program Director for the day. The winner may have privileges such as making daily announcements, greeting parents and providing feedback on program decisions.

3. Provide letter writing supplies to the participants and encourage them to begin writing persuasive letters to the current Program Director explaining why they would make a terrific replacement for a day. Encourage the participants to refer to the notes taken during your initial discussion.

4. Participants can proof each other's letters. Final copies should be well written with neat penmanship or typed.

Judges of Persuasive Letters

1. If you have the approval from the Program Director, announce to the participants that the judges will be the people giving up their jobs for the day.

2. On the other hand, if the participants will not really be taking on an actual job for the day, compile a panel of judges. The panel may include peers, parent volunteers, student council members or classroom teachers.

3. Present the judges with the entries. You may consider presenting them with an evaluation list with criteria agreed upon by the participants. The information compiled from their brainstorm list works great as a judging criteria.

When the Winner is Announced...

1. Announce the winner, or winners! This can be as elaborate or as simple as the participants decide to make it.

2. If the winner really can fill in a position for the day, be sure to announce the date when announcing the winner. This will give the participants something to prepare for and look forward to.

Extension Ideas

✎ Before the participants write their letters, have the Program Director visit to explain the job duties.

✎ Have participants research successful persuasive letters online.

✎ Have parents and community members visit to tell about their jobs in a mini-career fair.

✎ Have other children film the winner working as the Program Director.

✎ Have participants verbally present their entries to judges and other audience members.

✎ Try School Principal for the day.

"Content Standards"
Writing Strategies
Organization and Focus
✎ Create multiple-paragraph expository compositions:
  a. Engage the interest of the reader and state a clear purpose.
  b. Develop the topic with supporting details and precise verbs, nouns, and adjectives to paint a visual image in the mind of the reader.
  c. Conclude with a detailed summary linked to the purpose of the composition.

Evaluation and Revision
✎ Revise writing to improve the organization and consistency of ideas within and between paragraphs.
✎ Write expository compositions:
  a. State the thesis or purpose.
  b. Explain the situation.
  c. Follow an organizational pattern. appropriate to the type of composition.
  d. Offer persuasive evidence to validate arguments and conclusions as needed.

11 to 14

Reading to the Little Guys

Staff Role and Space

Staff will explain process and supervise children. Either staff or older children can plan for when, where and how they will have younger children join them for a special story time.
Quiet reading area.

Time

Prep Time: Making arrangements to match the older participants with the younger children.
Minimum Time Needed:
   Three 45-minute sessions:
      - Introduction of activity
      - Preparing for reading sessions
      - Reading to younger children

Supplies

Story Books
Younger and Older Children

Adaptation/Modifications

✎ Encourage the older children to work with younger children who share the same home language. Provide them with books in their shared language.
✎ If multiple daily visits are possible, encourage older children to read chapter books to the younger children. Make sure that the older readers know how to ask questions or summarize what has been read before to re-familiarize the children with the story.
✎ Let the younger children choose the books that they want read to them.

Purpose

For older participants to have the opportunity to read aloud to a younger child and learn about speech delivery and holding the interest of an audience.

Directions

Preparing Before Joining Younger Children

1. Have the older children gather together and discuss how and when they will read to younger children.

2. Provide them with a large variety of books to choose to read with the young children. They should choose ones they enjoy and are excited about reading.

3. Have the older children read through the book before sharing it with the younger children.

4. If possible, assign a younger child to each older child in advance. After a few practice sessions, some of the older children may enjoy reading to small groups of younger children.

Hints For Reading to Young Children

1. Be familiar with the individual characters and use different voices for them.

2. Pause between pages to look at pictures and discuss them with the young children.

3. Be ready to answer the younger child's questions and listen to their predictions while reading the story.

4. Have a simple project associated with the book to work on with the child after reading. (See examples)

5. Remember, engaging the child in the book will help instill a love of reading that will last a life time!

> Psst ...
> Both the older children and the younger children benefit greatly from this activity!

Simple Follow-Up Activities

Younger children will enjoy these simple activities to complete after a story is read to them by an older child:

✎ Draw a picture of your favorite character and write why they were your favorite.

✎ Make a book mark! See page 24 for our simple book mark activity.

✎ Together, act out one scene from the story.

✎ Write a poem about the characters, setting or a scene of the story.

✎ Ask the child to make up and tell you another story with the same characters as the book you shared.

Favorite Books To Read Aloud
Also check out the suggested books in the activities for 5-8 year olds

✎ *My Friend Rabbit* , **Eric Rohmann**

✎ *The Three Pigs,* **David Wiesner**

✎ *Click, Clack, Moo: Cows That Type,* **Betsy Lewin**

✎ *Jesse Bear, What Will You Wear?,* **Nancy Carlston**

✎ *Harlem A Poem,* **Walter Dean Myers**

✎ *Chicka Chicka Boom Boom*, **Bill Martin**

✎ *In the Small, Small Pond* , **Denise Fleming**

✎ *Good-Night Owl*, **Pat Hutchins**

✎ *The Story of Jumping Mouse,* **John Steptoe**

✎ *The Girl Who Loved Wild Horses,* **Paul Goble**

Extension Ideas

✎ Plan regularly scheduled visits between these two groups of children.

✎ Host an evening story hour and invite the younger children to attend in their pajamas!

✎ Plan a trip to the local library with younger and older children.

✎ Have the older children take dictation from the younger children and create a book together.

✎ Check with your local library for a program that helps adults learn to read and inquire about the middle school children assisting.

✎ Encourage the children to create a Little/Big Buddy Pen Pal group!

"Content Standards"
Listening and Speaking
Delivery of Oral Communication

✎ Organize information to achieve particular purposes by matching the message, vocabulary, voice modulation, expression, and tone to the audience and purpose.

✎ Use precise language, action verbs, sensory details, appropriate and colorful modifiers, and the active rather than the passive voice in ways that enliven oral presentations.

✎ Use audience feedback.

11 to 14

Round Robin Writing

Staff Role and Space

Staff introduce different topics, prepare writing prompts and provide support. This activity can be done anywhere and anytime. This is a great activity during homework time if there are no assignments.

Time

Prep Time: Time to gather materials
Minimum time needed for each writing session:
- 5 minutes to introduce writing ideas
- no more than 20 minutes of writing time
- 1-2 minutes per group to read their stories

Supplies

Writing prompts:
- incomplete sentence lists
- engaging pictures

Sets of pens with different color inks
Lined paper
Construction paper (optional)
Markers, colored pencils, other decorating materials (optional)

Adaptation/Modifications

✎ Allow the participants to help each other with spelling and writing, but make sure the ideas are elicited from each person in the group.
✎ Allow participants to write in their home language.

Purpose

To practice writing narratives and build relationships between participants.

Directions

Stage One: Getting Started

1. Divide the participants into groups of no more than four people and no less than two.

2. Make sure each member of the group has a pen with different colored ink. The group should have only one piece of paper for the entire group.

3. Provide each group with a writing prompt. See suggested prompts on the next page.

4. One person in the group starts writing. That person writes a sentence with his or her colored pen then passes the paper to the next person, who writes a sentence with his or her colored pen, and then passes it on. The group continues to take turns writing sentences until time is called.

5. After time is called, each group takes turns reading their stories aloud to the others.

Stage Two: Refining the narrative (Do not rush into Stage Two. Have the groups do a few Round Robin sessions over a couple of weeks before introducing stage two.)

1. Talk to participants about what makes a good narrative:
Setting:
    ✎ main characters
    ✎ time
    ✎ place of the story action
Initiating Event (Problem): An action or happening that sets up a problem or dilemma for the story.
Events: Sequence of actions that lead to a solution.
Solution: The result of the events.
Reaction: A response by the main character to the consequence.

Psst ...
Only correct spelling and grammar if there is going to be an audience for the story other than the group.

2. Encourage the participants to be conscious of the elements of a good narrative as they write their next story. They might want to discuss their setting, problem and solution before they start writing, letting the event, between the beginning and the end, happen spontaneously.

3. Have them follow the same process as Stage One.

4. After they have finished writing, have them go back and find all the nouns and if they do not have a description word or phrase for that noun, add one. Do the same thing for the verbs.

Warning: It is more important that the participants have fun with their stories than to get all the elements perfectly correct. If you find that the groups are becoming discouraged or "thinking" too hard about what they are writing, encourage them to just let go of any of the pre-plans they have made before writing, and just get the ideas down.

Writing Prompts

✎ Paste, on to construction paper, pictures cut from magazines or old calendars that might arouse feelings: beautiful sunsets, misty nights, children playing, sporty cars. Pass the pictures around for the participants to use as stimulus for their writing.

✎ Provide the first line for a story leaving off the ending:

> It was a dark and stormy night.....
>
> The heavy steps behind him stopped....
>
> The noisy party seemed to go on and on ....
>
> As the boys faced each other, they smiled....
>
> The small yapping dog would not .....
>
> The sleek, fast car swerved in front of ...
>
> From way above the street, the ....

Extension Ideas

✎ Have a short story competition with a panel of community members to judge the best story.

✎ Make a book of short stories using one of the book making ideas such as the hinged books in "Riddle Books" or the bound book in "Cook Books" activities. Donate the books to the after-school library.

✎ Explore different genres of short stories: science fiction, mystery, romance. Have the participants write Round Robin stories in each genre.

✎ Read the stories to younger children. Perhaps these readings could be part of the "Adopt a Fifth Grader" session as described on page 120.

"Content Standards"
Writing Applications
✎ Write narratives
✎ Establish and develop a plot and setting.
✎ Employ narrative and descriptive strategies.
Written and Oral English Conventions
✎ Students write and speak with a command of standard English conventions appropriate to their grade level.

11 to 14

Singing the Bios

Staff Role and Space

Staff will provide initial instruction and support as needed.

This can be done in any space but a quiet area for the interviewing process is recommended.

Time

Prep Time: none needed
Minimum Time Needed:
Two 45-minute sessions

Supplies

Pencils
Paper
Participants will enjoy using background music in their presentations. (optional)

Adaptation/Modifications

✎ Encourage participants to assist one another with the writing section of this activity.

✎ Do not check for spelling and grammar. It is important for the participants to express themselves verbally.

Purpose

For participants to interview each other and prepare a biography outline to be presented to the group.

Directions

1. Discuss biographies with the participants as books or stories written about a specific person. Have them share favorite biographies they have read, or ones they would like to read.

2. Explain to the participants that they will be interviewing a partner and then writing a short biography of that person in the form of a song or rap.

3. Have the group break into pairs or small groups. For interviewing question ideas, please see activity *My Private Thoughts: Journal Writing* on page 140.

4. The participants will take notes during the interview. Allow plenty of time for interviews and encourage participants to learn new things about one another.

5. When the interviews are complete, the participants will write a biography in the form of a song, rap or poem. Allow creativity and explain that the biographies will be presented to the large group.

6. Schedule a time for participants to present and share their biographies.

Psst ...
After a few sessions, this activity will take on a life of it's own as participants will break into rap-bios of one another and maybe autobiographies!

Psst ...
There are popular entertainers who have been negative when singing information about others in this format. It is advisable that staff be watchful of such tendencies and set clear expectations with participants.

Interview Question Ideas

✎ Where were you born?

✎ What are your plans after you graduate?

✎ Tell me one secret about you no one knows.

✎ What would you like to do to improve the world?

✎ If you were to run for Mayor, what would your main campaign points be?

My Guy Ace
by Fred

I've never told him this to his face,

I guess because it makes me not cool,

The coolest name, for the coolest guy, Ace

In his dream, he makes the girls drool.

Born in another state, too far away to matter,

He's here to stay with us.

And that's what really matters.

He lives with Ms. Ace, his Mother

And has Ty, that's his little brother.

You'll find him skating at the park,

All day until way past dark

He hopes to be a lawyer, winning case after case,

With a name like Ace, he'll win any race.

Extension Ideas

✎ Provide participants with a variety of biographies appropriate to their reading level.

✎ Invite a local journalist or journalism students from a university to visit and share interviewing skills with participants.

✎ Check favorite magazines of the participants for suggested interview questions.

✎ Host an evening event for families and friends to enjoy presentations of biographies.

"Content Standards"
Writing Applications
Write Narratives

✎ Establish and develop a plot and setting and present a point of view that is appropriate to the stories.

✎ Include sensory details and concrete language to develop plot and character.

✎ Use a range of narrative devices.

Listening and Speaking
Comprehension

✎ Select a focus, an organizational structure, and a point of view, matching the purpose, message, occasion, and vocal modulation to the audience.

✎ Emphasize salient points to assist the listener in following the main ideas and concepts.

✎ Use effective rate, volume, pitch, and tone and align nonverbal elements to sustain audience interest and attention.

11 to 14

Star Showcase

Staff Role and Space

Adults will provide supplies, suggested activities and supervision.
A theater or stage area.

Time

Prep Time: Time to gather materials
Minimum time needed:

At least six 45-minute sessions
- Discuss activity and begin initial plans
- Assign roles, plan and rehearse
- Plan, create flyers, posters, programs and rehearse
- Rehearse, finish posters, programs and flyers
- Set up theatre area and rehearse
- Rehearse and apply finishing touches

The determination on the amount of time needed will be based on the size of your group and how much of a production they want to present.

Supplies

A white board, chalkboard or flip chart
Butcher paper, for banners
Poster board, for signs
Paint & Markers
Activity Planning Sheet. p. 185

Adaptation/Modifications

✎ Encourage children to perform in their home language.
✎ Provide participants with challenges as well as support by pairing them up with others of varying talents and strengths.

Purpose

For participants to plan, organize, prepare publicity for, perform and present a talent show.

Directions

1. Discuss with participants the idea of presenting a *Star Showcase*, a talent show. Inspire and encourage conversations with leads such as:

✎ What type of talent can we showcase?
✎ What do we need to think about and include when planning a *Star Showcase*?
✎ What about the program that lists the acts?
✎ Who should we invite as an audience?

2. Have the participants brainstorm everyone's ideas concerning what the *Star Showcase* will include and how it will be presented. Record this information on the blackboard or flip chart.

3. Break the duties into committees. Include:

✎ Promoters
✎ Sign Makers
✎ Program Designers
✎ Talent Schedulers
✎ Set Up Committee
✎ Clean Up Committee
✎ Decorating Committee
✎ Emcees
✎ Refreshment Committee

Psst...
Emphasize the importance of all roles to participants. Whether they are an act, a curtain puller or a program lay-out specialist, all the participants have an important role.

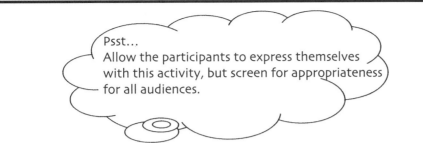

Psst...
Allow the participants to express themselves with this activity, but screen for appropriateness for all audiences.

4. The committees will have to schedule their time and devise their work plan. Some groups may need more direct supervision and support from adults; others may need minimal adult input.

5. As a large group, have the participants create a large scale action plan. Their action plan may follow the following format:

Duty	Supplies Needed	Who's Duty	Date to Complete	Update	Check In, Report
Make tickets	Computer, stationery	Promoting Comm.	1 week before show	On task	✔
Reserve multi-purpose room	Calendar with proposed dates	Scheduling Comm.	ASAP	Reserved for first Thurs. in June	✔
Write letters for donations of supplies	Stationery, writing supplies, list of potential donors	Refreshment Comm.	2 weeks before show	Asked director for list of parents and local businesses	✔

6. Be sure to include a writing activity for each committee. Writing thank you cards, acknowledgements, programs, signs and participant certificates are ideas to include.

7. Enjoy the collaborations of the different committees and allow them to be Stars!

Recommended Books

✎ *Who Says I Can't,* **Mary C. Robbin**

✎ *Elizabeth's Wish,* **Deborah M. Newton Chocolate**

✎ *Spotlight on Cody,* **Betsy Duffey**

Extension Ideas

✎ Take the show on the road! Visit centers with younger children or senior centers and present your Star Showcase.

✎ Invite your local community access television station to record and televise your show.

✎ Video tape your show and have a special viewing for the participants to enjoy.

✎ Have the participants write a follow up newsletter showcasing the highlights of the Star Showcase.

✎ Combine the Star Showcase with a simple spaghetti dinner as a fundraiser.

"Content Standards"
Writing Strategies
Research and Technology
✎ Create documents by using word-processing skills and publishing programs.
Written Language Conventions
Grammar
✎ Demonstrate the mechanics of writing and appropriate English usage.
Spelling
✎ Spell derivatives correctly by applying the spellings of bases and affixes.

11 to 14

Teen Mags Starring "Yours Truly"

Staff Role and Space

Adults will provide supplies, suggested activities and supervision.
An art activity area works great.

Time

Prep Time: Time to gather materials, especially magazines
Minimum time needed:
    At least two 45-minute sessions

Supplies

Variety of teen magazines to cut up
Scissors
Glue sticks
Large construction paper or poster boards
Markers
Rulers
Miscellaneous art supplies, such as glitter, paints, or stickers (optional)
Instant camera (optional)

Adaptation/Modifications

✎ Create a balanced magazine staff including writers, photographers, editors and layout specialist.
✎ If younger children are doing this activity, it is advisable to use other types of magazines like nature or sport magazines.

Purpose

For participants to read and discuss popular culture materials and creatively write their personal entries.

Directions

1. Have the children divide into groups of approximately five. These groups will work together to create a teen publication based on themselves, celebrities or imaginary individuals.

2. Discuss the content of the popular teen magazines with the children. Leading questions may include:

> ✎ What types of situations are the celebrities often shown in?
>
> ✎ How do their lives differ from yours?
>
> ✎ If you were a celebrity, what would your claim to fame be?
>
> ✎ Would you like to be a reporter or a photographer to the stars?

3. Using the magazines as guides, the children will discuss what they want their magazine, or poster, to include and what it will look like. Let their creativity take over!

Psst...
Allow middle school children to 'act their age' and provide privacy from younger children while they work on their projects.

Psst...
You will be pleasantly surprised with these finished projects. Try to hang on to a few for samples!

4. Choices of layouts and topics may include:
   - ✎ A Typical Day in Our Lives – Daily Newspaper
   - ✎ The Main Feature – A Movie Poster
   - ✎ Our Times – A Weekly or Monthly News Publication
   - ✎ The Road to Our Success – A look at where we will be 10 or 20 years from now and how we will get there.
   - ✎ At Your Request – A brochure for our business, highlighting our talents

The participants will be much more creative and 'hip' with their titles and formats. These are suggestions to help get them started.

5. Articles or features to consider:
   - ✎ An Advice Column
   - ✎ A Fashion Alert
   - ✎ Upcoming Events
   - ✎ Feature Articles
   - ✎ Entertainment Guide

6. Children may cut up the teen magazines and use them for headlines, pictures or many other imaginative ways.

7. When projects are complete, allow time for participants to present and share their efforts.

Extension Ideas

- ✎ Visit a local newspaper office or printing press.
- ✎ Have a local photographer visit.
- ✎ Provide children with disposable cameras or a Polaroid camera to take their own pictures to add to their project.
- ✎ Have children write fan mail to their favorite celebrities. Fan club mailing addresses can be found online.
- ✎ Make this a regularly scheduled activity and make copies for a newsletter to share with families.
- ✎ Include these in your yearbook.
- ✎ Combine this activity with *Create Board Games* on page 78. The theme of the board game will be the same as the publication.

"Content Standards"

Reading Comprehension
Structural Features of Informational Materials
- ✎ Identify the structural features of popular media (e.g., newspapers, magazines, online information) and use the features to obtain information.
- ✎ Analyze text that uses the compare-and-contrast organizational pattern.

Expository Critique
- ✎ Note instances of unsupported inferences, fallacious reasoning, persuasion, and propaganda in text.

Writing Strategies
Organization and Focus
- ✎ Choose the form of writing (e.g., personal letter, letter to the editor, review, poem, report, narrative) that best suits the intended purpose.

11 to 14

Time Capsule

Staff Role and Space

Staff should lead initial discussion and then support teams or individuals in the development of their ideas.

This activity can be done anywhere. You will have to have a place to store your container, so make sure it is a size that fits the area you have.

Time

Prep time: Time to get container and other materials.

Minimum time needed:
- Discussion of what should be placed in the capsule – 45 minutes
- Gathering of objects and writing of description of selections – Initially 45 minutes, but could go over the entire program year.
- Planning and celebrating the ceremony for closing the capsule – 45 minutes

Supplies

Waterproof and airtight container. The size will depend on how big you want to make your capsule.
Objects chosen by the participants
Paper and pen/pencils

Adaptation/Modifications

✎ Work in teams so that the child that can write well serves as the recorder.
✎ Younger children can dictate their descriptions.

Purpose

To practice writing descriptive paragraphs and autobiographical stories.

Directions

1. Discuss the idea of a time capsule. Why would you want to make one? How long might a time capsule stay closed? Who might want to open one? What would you want to see in a time capsule from the past?

2. Decide as a group the purpose for the time capsule. Who will be opening it? Some ideas include:

 ✎ Themselves a couple years in the future, or even at the end of the present year

 ✎ Elementary school children who are entering the middle school program

 ✎ Parents

 ✎ Unknown individuals in the future

3. Decide on what should go into the time capsule. If the time capsule is to represent the group as a whole, the whole group will have to approve the selection. If an individual time capsule, have each person describe to the others what they have included and why.

Psst ...
Research indicates that providing opportunities for ritual is important for the development of resiliency in children. Encourage the participants to experience this activity as something meaningful in their lives.

4. Have the participants write a description of each item and why they included it. You can have them do this as :

✎ an annotated list: each item's name with a short description

✎ a "catalogue": a picture of each item with a short description

✎ a narrative: a story of why each item was selected.

5. Impress on the participants that others will be reading what they have written, and so they need to spend time making sure that they have proper spelling, grammar and neat penmanship. Help them with drafts and re-writes.

6. Have the participants design a ceremony for the closing of the time capsule. For example, you can have each one write a short message to the opener of the capsules, then individually put it in the capsule, and then close it and quietly carry it to where it is going to be stored. It is important to impress on the participants a sense of seriousness attached to the ritual.

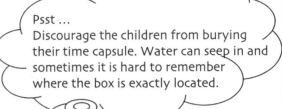

Psst …
Discourage the children from burying their time capsule. Water can seep in and sometimes it is hard to remember where the box is exactly located.

Ideas of Objects to Go Into Time Capsules

✎ Newspaper or magazine articles
✎ "Dear me" letters. Letters to yourself that you will read a couple of years or months into the future about what you are thinking about in the present time.
✎ Art objects made in the program
✎ Favorite menus or wrappers from snacks or candy
✎ Song lyrics
✎ Games or items that are popular to collect
✎ Photos of participants doing various activities
✎ Copies of the program rules
✎ Picture of popular clothes
✎ Suggestions for younger children who might be entering the program when the capsule is going to be opened

Objects to Avoid…

✎ Any food item unless it is freeze-dried
✎ Fragile items unless carefully wrapped
✎ If you plan to leave the time capsule closed for a long period of time (over 10 years), stay away from items that require an electronic playback device such video or audio tapes. For example, we do not know if VCR's will still be available 10 years from now.

Extension Ideas

✎ Make the development of a time capsule a ritual in your program. If you have young people who stay in your program over a couple of years, let them make one when they enter and then open it at a ceremony when they leave.
✎ Talk to a member of your local government, and arrange for a capsule to be placed in a community area with arrangements for it to be opened sometime in the future.
✎ Exchange capsules across sites at the end of the year. It is always exciting if the exchange can be with someplace far away, such as cross country or even in another country.
✎ Bring in art and auction catalogues and talk about how objects are described.

"Content Standards"
Writing:
✎ Revise writing for word choice: appropriate organization; consistent point of view; and transitions between paragraphs, passages and ideas.
Written and Oral English Language Conventions:
✎ Students write and speak with a command of standard English conventions appropriate to the grade level.

11
to
14

What's to Eat?: Making Cookbooks

Staff Role and Space

Staff should provide cookbooks, recipes, and other resources, and lead the initial discussion about recipes.

This activity can be done anywhere. In order to field test the recipes access to a kitchen is necessary.

Time

Prep Time: Time to gather materials
Minimum time needed:

Three 45 minute sessions – could take an entire semester.

- One session to make the cookbooks
- Two sessions to work on recipes

Supplies

Supplies listed in book-making directions
Various cookbooks and other cooking resources
Glossary of Cooking Terms
Thesaurus
Ingredients, cooking supplies to test recipes (optional)

Adaptation/Modifications

✎ Have the participants work in teams mixing different learning strengths including reading, writing, artistic and cooking skills.
✎ Take advantage of different ethnic backgrounds of the participants by encouraging them to bring in recipes from their background.
✎ If you do not have access to a kitchen, make your cookbook out of non-cook recipes.

Purpose

To write clear directions and appropriate descriptive language.

Directions

1. Talk to the participants about their favorite foods and share with them other foods that you will be introducing.

2. Have them select a dish they would like to know how to make and investigate different recipes using the resources you have provided.

3. Have them decide about the ingredients and the steps they plan to use to cook the food. Encourage them not to just copy the recipe, but to think the process out for themselves.

4. Lead a brainstorming session about words they could use to describe food textures, tastes and other related areas. For example:

      smooth: velvety, creamy, soft, rich

5. Encourage them to look up interesting words in the thesaurus to describe their dishes for the description section of the recipe.

6. Have them complete the recipe worksheet provided on the next page.

7. After finishing the recipe worksheets, compile the recipes and make a bound book out of them following the directions found on page 192.

Psst...
Many after-school programs are required to reinforce good nutritional understanding. This is a great activity to help in this requirement.

(Reproducible on page 193)

Recipe Worksheet

Name of Dish
(Sentence or two describing the dish)

Ingredients:

Directions:

| Illustration |

Cost per Serving:

Nutritional Facts:

Background on the recipe:

Written by: _____

Suggested Resources

Check out the websites at the back of the book for a link to recipes for young people.

✎ *Clueless in the Kitchen: A Cookbook for Teens,* **Evelyn Raab and George Walker**

✎ *Cook and Learn: Pictorial Single Portion Recipes,* **B. Weith and T. Harms**

✎ *Kids Around the World Cook!: The Best Foods and Recipes from Many Lands,* **Arlette N. Braman**

✎ *Better Homes and Gardens New Junior Cookbook,* **Jennifer Dorland Darling**

Extension Ideas

✎ Join with your computer classes to work on layouts and desktop publishing to make your cookbooks.

✎ Join with your gardening program to use their produce to determine recipes.

✎ Decide on a cookbook theme such as ethnic cooking, cooking from the garden.

✎ Develop your cookbook as a product to sell. Join with or form a small business club to establish a company to sell the book.

✎ Invite a cook or visit a restaurant in the area. Have the participants interview cooks about how they use recipes.

✎ Invite parents in the community to share favorite foods and recipes.

✎ Invite the parents and community members in for a taste feast.

"Content Standards"
Reading
Vocabulary and Concept Development
✎ Recognize the origins and meanings of frequently used foreign words in English.
Structural Features of Informational Materials
✎ Locate information by using a variety of consumer, workplace, and public documents.
✎ Understand and explain the use of a simple mechanical device by following technical directions.
Writing
✎ Students write with a command of standard English conventions appropriate for the grade level.

11 to 14

Reproducible on p. 193

Writing Children's Books with a Message

Staff Role and Space

Staff will need to:
- *gather appropriate children's books for the participants to examine,*
- *lead the discussions as defined in the directions,*
- *arrange for an opportunity for the older children to read their books, and*
- *encourage and supervise the participants.*

This activity can be done anywhere. It works best in an area with few distractions and with access to some type of chart paper or board. There also needs to be an area to store the books as they are being developed.

Time

Prep Time: Time to gather the appropriate books and materials
Minimum time needed:
   At least five 45-minute sessions:
   - Discussion of the children's books
   - Writing first and second drafts of the book
   - Reading the books to the children
   - Discussion after the reading

Supplies

Many children's books about important life issues
Paper for both writing the drafts and the final copy
Material for drawing illustrations such as colored pencils, crayons, markers, stencils
Construction paper
Book-making materials (see suggested types in direction # 7)

Purpose

To practice reading and writing for a purpose, and to reinforce understanding of the elements of narratives.

Directions

1. Select a variety of children's books that relate to social issues such as divorce, death, violence and peer pressure. (Children's librarians should be able to assist in identifying these books.)

2. Divide the participants into groups of three. Ask the students to analyze the books for theme, character and authenticity of emotions.

3. Discuss in the groups whether the books provided helpful insights on how to handle such emotional topics. Also discuss what techniques the authors used to discuss these complicated topics in a way that children could understand them.

4. Brainstorm areas causing young children concern in their community. Discuss what would be appropriate language and presentation techniques for young children that they should include in their books.

5. Each group will then write a rough draft of a small, illustrated book on a topic which would be of interest to the children. Before beginning their writing have the students decide on a plan for completing the project including:
   - ✎ projected completion date,
   - ✎ listing of the tasks that need to be accomplished,
   - ✎ time lines, and
   - ✎ delegation of responsibilities.
(If participants are not familiar with planning strategies, the staff member might need to help them think through the steps that they should consider.)

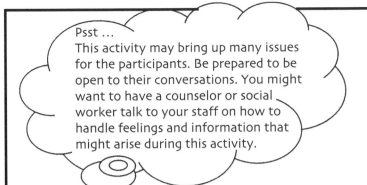

Psst ...
This activity may bring up many issues for the participants. Be prepared to be open to their conversations. You might want to have a counselor or social worker talk to your staff on how to handle feelings and information that might arise during this activity.

6. After they have written their drafts, trade the books amongst the groups. Have each team edit a book from another group.

7. After the books have been edited, have the groups make their final drafts with illustrations. Check the Riddle Book activity on page 102 or the directions for making a bound book found on page 192.

After the books are written...

8. The students will then read their books to small groups of elementary school-age children and lead a discussion about their book's topic.

9. After reading and discussing the book with the children, the groups can come back together and discuss how the elementary school-age children responded. They can analyze the responses to think about how they need to change their books to make them more effective. (Carry this project as far as the participants can tolerate. If they want to actually revise their book at this point, encourage them to do so.)

Resources

✎ *Storybooks for Tough Times,* **Laura Ann Campbell, Laura K. Campbell**

✎ *The Right Book, The Right Time: Helping Children Cope,* **Martha C. Grindler, Beverly D. Stratton, Michael C. McKenna**

** See the appendix for websites that have lists of children's books you can use to gather material for this activity. Remember that your best resource is the children's librarian in your public library.

Adaptation/Modifications

✎ Group the participants so that the different types of talents are represented including the ability to write, plan, draw etc.

✎ Allow the participants to write in the language they are most comfortable using. Encourage them to write the stories in the language of the children to whom they will be reading.

Extension Ideas

✎ Build a program library of books written by participants. Share the library with other sites.

✎ Invite a counselor to come in and discuss the issues found in the books with the participants.

✎ Provide child development information about the characteristics of young children. Check out videos that cover this area.

✎ Set up a buddy reading program. See the "Reading to the Little Guys" activity found on page 152.

"Content Standards"
Reading
Narrative Analysis
✎ Identify and analyze recurring themes.
Literary Criticism
✎ Analyze a range of responses to a literary work and determine the extent to which the literary elements in the work shaped those responses.
Writing
Write narratives that
✎ Develop a standard plot line.
✎ Reveal the significance of, or the writer's attitude about, the subject.
✎ Employ narrative and descriptive strategies.

11 to 14

<u>Appendices</u>

Glossary

Reproducibles

Resources

Glossary of Literacy Terms

(Only the most common word analysis terms are included in this glossary. Check the glossary in the book, *Words Their Way* by Donald R. Bear et al. for a more complete glossary of technical terms for word analysis.)

📖 **Affix:** A word part that is attached to either the beginning or ending of a word. (Prefixes and Suffixes.)

📖 **Blending:** Combining word parts together quickly so that the entire word is pronounced in a meaningful way. For example, /k/ /i/ /nd/ would be blended together to form the word *kind*.

📖 **Comprehension:** The act of constructing meaning from text. Includes strategies such as connecting what is being read to existing knowledge, visualizing, inferring, summarizing and evaluating.

📖 **Concept of Print:** The knowledge of how print is usually formatted. For example, the fact that in English, readers read from left to right, top to bottom; or that books have front and back covers; or the reasons for capitalization and punctuation.

📖 **Decoding:** A series of strategies used by readers to recognize and read written words in order to pronounce those words and give meaning to them. Word analysis is one example of decoding.

📖 **Expository or informational Text:** Text written to explain and convey information and details about a specific subject or topic.

📖 **Fluency:** Clear, easy and quick written or spoken expression of ideas with little need to rely on using word analysis strategies.

📖 **Genre:** Categories used to describe written fictional material based on their shared structure, organization, and or perspective. Examples of different genre are fiction, drama, poetry, fairy tales, science fiction, and short stories.

📖 **Grammar:** The system of rules that are used in spoken and written language that allow individuals who know the grammar to understand what is being communicated.

📖 **High Frequency Words:** Words that appear most frequently in written and spoken language. In English these words tend to be irregular and have to be learned by sight. Examples of high frequency words are *and, above, because*. See the appendix for a sight vocabulary list.

📖 **Literary Analysis:** The study or examination of a literary work.

📖 **Literary Criticism:** A judgment or evaluation of a literary work made after a literary analysis.

Fun Literacy Activities for After-School Programs

📖 **Narrative:** A story or narrated account of actual or fictional events. (See *expository writing* for its opposite.)

📖 **Persuasion:** A type of either oral or written composition whose purpose is to move a reader to belief and/or action.

📖 **Phonemic Awareness:** The knowledge that spoken words consist of a sequence of individual sounds, and the understanding that phonemes (speech sounds) can be rearranged and substituted to create new words. Skills involved in phonemic awareness include rhyming, blending, substitution etc.

📖 **Phonics:** A systematic system of teaching reading and spelling that stresses sound-symbol relationships through word analysis.

📖 **Punctuation:** The use of standard marks, such as periods, commas, in writing to clarify meaning and to provide some indication on how the written form would be spoken.

📖 **Retelling:** The oral or written paraphrasing of a story using the teller's own words.

📖 **Sentences:**
   - *Declarative*- a sentence that makes a statement
   - *Exclamatory* – a sentence that expresses a strong emotion
   - *Imperative* – a sentence that makes a command or request
   - *Interrogative* – a sentence that asks a question or makes an inquiry

📖 **Sight Word Vocabulary:** Words that are read automatically without needing to be analyzed. As we become more fluent readers, most words would be considered sight word vocabulary. However, at the early stages of reading, sight word vocabulary usually refers to those words found on lists of high frequency words.

📖 **Story grammar:** The elements of a fictional story. These elements usually consist of plot, setting, characters, conflict or problem, events or attempts for resolution, often a complication and solution. The theme of the story is also part of the story grammar.

📖 **Story Sequence:** The order of the events in a narrative.

📖 **Theme:** The message about life or human nature that is the focus of the story.

📖 **Word Analysis or Word Attack:** Strategies readers perform when they do not instantly recognize a word. These strategies include left-to-right blending of sounds, phonics, structural analysis and using rules of syllabication.

📖 **Word Families:** A collection of words that share common spelling rimes (the part of the syllable that consists of a vowel and any consonant sound that comes after it.) For example, /at/ would be the rime for the word family: *bat, cat, fat, hat, flat.*

Reproducibles

Age 5-8 activities

1. List of Feelings
2. Blends and Digraphs
3. Word Families
4. Sight Vocabulary List
5. Creature Features Web
6. Aesop's Fables
7. Three Little Monkey's Song Lyrics
8. Making a Movie Worksheet
9. Common Tongue Twisters

Age 9-10 activities

1. Directions for clapping game, "Long Legged Sailor and his Wife"
2. "Do I have a Dream for You" Speech Outline
3. Fortunate Cookie Recipe

Age 11-14 activities

1. Activity Action Plan Form
2. Example of Codes
3. "Defending Your Life" Speech Outline
4. "I am…" Poem Format
5. Multicultural Game Worksheet
6. Journal Prompts
7. List of Word Parts
8. Directions for Making Books with Bindings
9. Recipe Worksheet

Feeling Words List

Words that express positive feelings

accepting	comfortable	fascinated	loved	serene
adequate	compassionate	fortunate	loving	spirited
affectionate	content	free	lucky	super
amazed	confident	fulfilled	merry	respected
animated	considerate	generous	optimistic	safe
appreciated	curious	glad	peaceful	surprised
attracted	daring	grateful	playful	sympathetic
befriended	delighted	great	pleased	tender
blessed	determined	happy	passionate	terrific
bold	encourage	helpful	proud	thankful
brave	eager	high	quiet	trusted
calm	ecstatic	hopeful	refreshed	thrilled
capable	elated	important	relaxed	understanding
certain	energetic	inspired	relieved	valued
cheerful	enthusiastic	interested	satisfied	wonderful
clever	excited	joyful	secure	
courageous	exuberant	kind	sensitive	

Words that express negative feelings

abandoned	defeated	grief	menaced	startled
angry	dejected	guilty	miserable	surprised
afraid	deprived	hateful	mixed-up	suspicious
aggressive	desperate	heartbroken	nervous	tearful
alienated	different	helpless	nosy	tense
alone	disappointed	hostile	overwhelmed	terrible
annoyed	disillusioned	humiliated	pained	terrified
anxious	disinterested	hurt	panic	tired
apprehensive	discouraged	impulsive	persecuted	threatened
ashamed	disgusting	incapable	powerless	tormented
awful	dissatisfied	infuriate	preoccupied	trapped
bad	distrustful	intimidated	pushy	troubled
betrayed	distressed	insecure	put-down	uncertain
bitter	doubtful	insignificant	rejected	uneasy
bored	dull	irritated	resentful	unhappy
bugged	embarrassed	isolated	restless	unloved
burdened	empty	jealous	scared	unpleasant
caught	envious	left out	shocked	upset
cheated	exhausted	lonely	shaky	unsettled
confused	fearful	lost	shy	unsure
concerned	foolish	lousy	skeptical	uptight
cowardly	frightened	mad	sorrowful	wary
crushed	frustrate	melancholy	squeezed	weary

Consonant Blends and Digraphs

Blends

Consists of two or more letters that must be combined to arrive at the correct pronunciation. The letters cannot be sounded out separately for proper pronunciation.

Two-letter initial consonant blends:

s- blends	-r blends	-l blends	t- blends	qu-blends
sc - scale	br - broom	bl - block	tw - twelve	qu-queen
sk - skin	cr - crutch	cl - clock		
sm - smell	dr - drink	fl - flag		
sn - snail	fr - frog	gl - glass		
sp - spool	gr - grape	pl - plane		
st - stairs	pr - prize	sl - slide		
sw - swing	tr - train			

Three -letter initial consonant blends:

scr - screen	spr - spring	str - string	thr - thread	spl-splash

Digraph

Combination of two letters that create one sound when prounced.

(t)ch	branch, chest, church, scratch, much, chop
sh	ash, trash, brush, shot, shell, dish
th	that, bath, thunder, father, smooth, think, thing
ng	hang, king, strong, sting, spring, swing, song, thing
wh	when, whip, whale, white, whisper, while
kn	knock, knot, knee, knife, knit, knob, kneel
ph	photo, orphan, gopher, graph, phone, trophy
wr	write, wrap, wrong, wrist, wreck, wrinkle, wreath, wrote
gh	ghost, ghetto, ghoul
gh	tough, rough, laugh

Sight Vocabulary List

a	cold	grow	may	said	too
about	come	had	me	saw	try
after	could	has	much	say	two
again	cut	have	must	see	under
all	did	he	my	seven	up
always	do	help	myself	shall	upon
am	does	her	never	she	us
an	done	here	new	show	use
and	don't	him	no	sing	very
any	down	his	not	sit	walk
are	draw	hold	now	six	want
around	drink	hot	of	sleep	warm
as	eat	how	off	small	was
ask	eight	hurt	old	so	wash
at	every	I	on	some	we
ate	fall	if	once	soon	well
away	far	in	one	start	went
be	fast	into	only	stop	were
because	find	is	open	take	what
been	first	it	or	tell	when
before	five	its	our	ten	where
best	fly	jump	out	thank	which
better	for	just	over	that	white
big	found	keep	own	the	who
black	four	kind	pick	their	why
blue	from	know	play	them	will
both	full	laugh	please	then	wish
bring	funny	let	pretty	there	with
brown	gave	light	pull	these	work
but	get	like	put	they	would
buy	give	little	ran	think	write
by	go	live	read	this	yellow
call	goes	long	red	those	yes
came	going	look	ride	three	you
can	good	made	right	to	you
carry	got	make	round	today	
clean	green	many	run	together	

Common Word Families

-ack: back, hack, lack, pack, quack, rack, sack, tack, black, clack, crack, knack, shack, slack, smack, snack, stack, track whack

- ail: bail, fail, hail, jail, mail, nail, pail, quail, rail, sail, tail, wail, flail, frail, snail, trail

- ain: ;ain, main, pain, rain, vain, brain, chain , drain, gain, plain, slain, Spain, sprain, stain, strain, train

-ake: bake, cake, fake, lake, make, quake, rake, take, wake, brake, drake, flake, shake, snake, stake, sake

- ale: bale, dale, gale, hale, male, pale, sale, tale, scale, shale, stale, whale

-ame: came, dame, fame, game, lame, name, same, tame, blame, flame, frame, shame

- an: ban, can, fan, man, pan, ran, tan, van, bran, clan, flan, plan, scan, span, than

-ank: bank, dank, hank, lank, sank, tank, yank, blank, clank, crank, drank, flank, plank, prank, shrank, spank, thank

- ap: gap, lap, map, nap, rap, sap, tap, yap, chap, clap, flap, scrap, slap, snap, strap, trap, wrap

-ash: bash, cash, crash, dash, gash, hash, lash, mash, rash, sash, brash, clash, flash, slash, smash, stash, thrash, trash

- at: bat, cat, fat, gnat, hat, mat, pat, rat, sat, tat, vat, brat, chat, flat, that

- ate: date, fate, gate, hate, late, mate, rate, crate, grate, plate, skate, state

- aw: caw, gnaw, jaw, law, paw, raw, saw, claw, draw, flaw, slaw, squaw, straw

- ay: bay, day, gay, hay, jay, lay, may, pay, ray, say, way, bray, clay, ray, gray, play, pray, slay, pray, stay, stray, sway, tray

-eat: beat, feat, heat, meat, neat, peat, seat, bleat, cheat, cleat, pleat, treat, wheat

-ell: bell, cell, dell, dwell, fell, jell, knell, sell, tell, well, yell, quell, shell, smell, spell

-est: best, guest, jest, lest, nest, pest, rest, test, vest, west, zest, blest, chest, crest, quest, wrest

-ice: dice, ice, lice, mice, nice, rice, vice, price, slice, spice, splice, twice, thrice

-ick: kick, lick, pick, quick, sick, tick, wick, brick, chick, click, flick, slick, stick, thick, trick

-ide: bide, hide, ride, side, tide, wide, bride, chide, glide, pride, slide, snide, stride

-ight: knight, light, might, night, right, sight, tight, blight, bright, flight, fright, plight, slight

- in: bin, din, fin, gin, kin, pin, sin, tin, win, chin, grin, shin, skin, spin, thin, twin

-ine: dine, fine, line, mine, nine, pine, tine, vine, wine, brine, shine, shrine, spine, swine, whine

-ing: bing, ding, king, ping, ring, sing, wing, zing, bring, cling, fling, sling, spring, sting, string, swing, thing, wring

-ink: kink, link, mink, pink, rink, sink, wink, blink, brink, chink, clink, drink, shrink, slink, stink, think

- ip: dip, hip, lip, nip, rip, sip, tip, zip, blip, chip, clip, drip, flip, grip, ship, skip, slip, snip, strip, trip, whip

- it: bit, fit, hit, it, kit, lit, pit, sit, wit, flit, grit, knit, quit, skit, slit, spit, split, twit

-ock: dock, hock, knock, lock, mock, rock, sock, tock, block, clock, crock, flock, frock, shock, smock, stock

-oke: joke, poke, woke, yoke, broke, choke, smoke, spoke, stoke, stroke

-op: cop, hop, mop, pop, sop, top, chop, crop, drop, flop, plop, prop, shop, slop, stop

-ore: bore, core, fore, gore, more, pore, sore, tore, wore, chore, score, shore, snore, spore, store, swore

-ot: cot, dot, got, hot, jot, knot, lot, not, pot, rot, tot, blot, clot, plot, shot, slot, spot, trot,

-uck: buck, duck, luck, muck, puck, suck, tuck, cluck, pluck, shuck, stuck, struck, truck

-ug: bug, dug, hug, jug, lug, mug, pug, rug, tug, chug, drug, plug, shrug, slug, smug, snug, thug

-ump: bump, dump, hump, jump, lump, pump, chump, clump, frump, grump, plump, slump, stump, thump, trump

-unk: bunk, dunk, funk, hunk, junk, punk, sunk, chunk, flunk, plunk, shrunk, skunk, slunk, spunk, stunk, trunk

My Creature

Name: _____

Brainstorm ideas for each circle. Write down one or two words on each line.

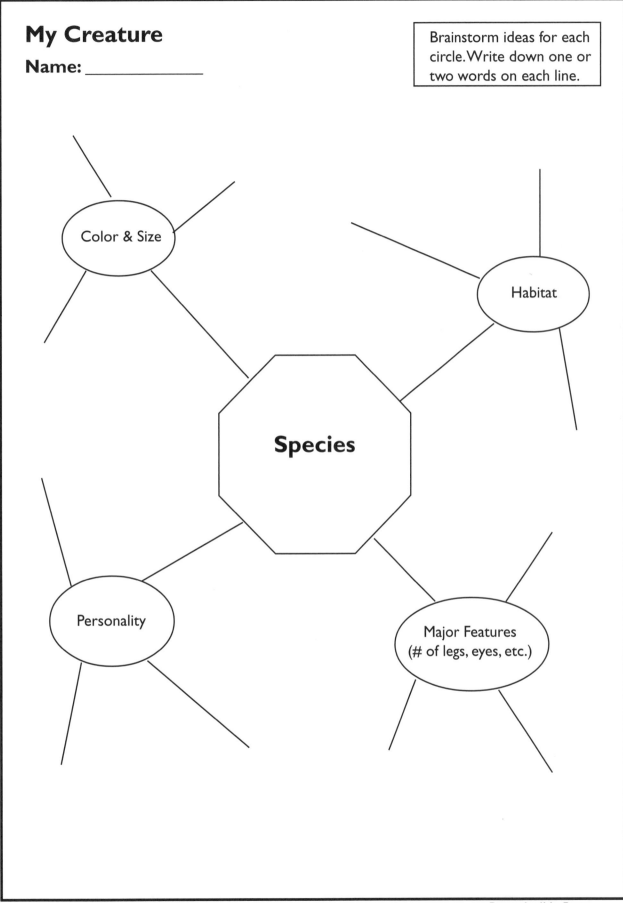

Color & Size

Habitat

Species

Personality

Major Features
(# of legs, eyes, etc.)

Aesop's Fables

The Lion and the Mouse

Once when a Lion was asleep a little Mouse began running up and down upon him; this soon wakened the Lion, who placed his huge paw upon him, and opened his big jaws to swallow him. "Pardon, O King," cried the little Mouse: "forgive me this time, I shall never forget it: who knows but what I may be able to do you a turn some of these days?" The Lion was so tickled at the idea of the Mouse being able to help him that he lifted up his paw and let him go. Some time after the Lion was caught in a trap, and the hunters who desired to carry him alive to the King, tied him to a tree while they went in search of a wagon to carry him on. Just then the little Mouse happened to pass by, and seeing the sad plight, in which the Lion was, went up to him and soon gnawed away the ropes that bound the King of the Beasts. "Was I not right?" said the little Mouse.

MORAL: Little friends may prove great friends.

The Ant and the Grasshopper

In a field one summer's day a Grasshopper was hopping about, chirping and singing to his heart's content. An Ant passed by, bearing along with great toil an ear of corn she was taking to the nest.

"Why not come and chat with me," said the Grasshopper, "instead of toiling and working in that way?"

"I am helping to lay up food for the winter," said the Ant, "and recommend you to do the same."

"Why bother about winter?" said the Grasshopper; we have got plenty of food at present." But the Ant went on her way and continued her work. When the winter came the Grasshopper had no food and found himself dying of hunger, while every day he saw the ants distributing corn and grain from the stores they had collected in the summer. Then the Grasshopper knew:

MORAL: It is best to prepare for the days of necessity.

Three Little Monkeys

Three little monkeys jumping on the bed

One fell off and bumped his head

So Momma called the doctor and the doctor said

"No more monkeys jumping on the bed!"

Two little monkeys jumping on the bed

One fell off and bumped his head

So Momma called the doctor and the doctor said

"No more monkeys jumping on the bed!"

One little monkey jumping on the bed

He fell off and bumped his head

So Momma called the doctor and the doctor said

"No more monkeys jumping on the bed!"

No little monkeys jumping on the bed

None fell off and bumped his head

So Momma called the doctor and the doctor said

"Put those monkeys back in bed!"

Making a Movie

Imagine that you are a screenwriter. Your job is to plan a film version of the book that you have just read. Follow these steps:

1. **Name:** What name will you be giving the movie?

   _____

2. **Who would you cast in the roles of the main characters?**

Main character	Actors
1. _____	_____
2. _____	_____
3. _____	_____
4. _____	_____

3. **Where would you film your movie?** List some places where you would film the different scenes.

   - _____
   - _____
   - _____

4. **Mood and Atmosphere:** List some sound effects, music for the background of the movie.

   - _____
   - _____
   - _____
   - _____

For activity on pages 64-65

Tongue Twisters

Peter Piper picked a peck of pickled peppers.
Did Peter Piper pick a peck of pickled peppers?
If Peter Piper picked a peck of pickled peppers,
Where's the peck of pickled peppers Peter Piper picked?

A big black bug bit a big black bear,
Made the big black bear bleed blood.

She sells sea shells by the sea shore.
The shells she sells are surely seashells.
So if she sells shells on the seashore,
I'm sure she sells seashore shells.

How much wood would a woodchuck chuck
if a woodchuck could chuck wood?
He would chuck, he would, as much as he could,
and chuck as much wood as a woodchuck would
if a woodchuck could chuck wood.

One-liners:

Toy boat. Toy boat. Toy boat.

Three free throws.

Knapsack straps.

A noisy noise annoys an oyster.

Fat frogs flying past fast.

Which wristwatches are Swiss wristwatches?

We surely shall see the sun shine soon.

Moose noshing much mush.

Black bug's blood.

Rubber baby buggy bumper

Long Legged Sailor and his Wife

Have you ever, ever, ever
In your long-legged life
Seen a long-legged sailor
With a long-legged wife?

No, I've never, ever, ever
in my long-legged life
Seen a long-legged sailor
with a long-legged wife.

Following verses: Repeat but substitute for long-legged
Verse 2: short-legged
Verse 3: bow-legged
Verse 4: pigeon-toed
Verse 5: chicken-clawed
Verse 6: pointed-headed

Hand Movements

Basic Movement

Line 1: Hand slap knees, clap one's own hands together, cross clap one hand with partner, clap one's own hand, cross clap other hand to partner's hand.
Line 2: Clap one's own hand, clap one's own hand, cross clap hands with partner,
Line 3: Clap one's own hand, cross clap hands with partner, clap one's own hand.
Line 4: Cross slap your partner's hand, Clap one's own hand, clap both of partner's hands together palms out, fingers pointing up.

Different motions occur in the different verses. Substitute the following motions for the appropriate phrases:

1. long-legged - hold hands stretched out wide in front of body, chest high with palms turned facing each other

2. short-legged - hold hands stretched out a little bit apart in front of body, chest high with palms inward

3. bow-legged - make fists with both hands and hold hands under arm pits

4. pigeon-toed - place knuckles of clinched fists about chest high together in front of body

5. chicken-clawed - make the hands form claws about chest height in front of the body

6. pointed- headed - hands over head with extended finger tips touching together

Do I Have a Dream for You!
Speech Outline

Position Statement: The job that I would like is
_____. I would like you to help me by_____.

Reason: _____
Explanation:

Reason: _____
Explanation:

Reason: _____
Explanation:

Conclusion:

Fortunately/Unfortunately Cookie Recipe

- Preheat oven to 325 degrees

- Ingredients:

  1/2 cup flour
  1/3 cup sugar
  1 Tablespoon cornstarch
  1/2 teaspoon salt
  1/4 cup melted butter or margarine
  4 egg whites
  2 Tablespoons milk
  2 teaspoons almond extract

- Combine flour, sugar, cornstarch and salt.

- In a separate bowl, beat butter, egg whites, milk and almond extract until smooth.

- Drop dough by tablespoons, 3 inches apart, onto greased cookie sheets.

- Bake 9-10 minutes, or until golden brown, on middle oven rack.

- Remove from cookie sheet immediately with spatula, onto waxed paper.

- Immediately, set one FORTUNATELY or UNFORTUNATELY strip of paper in center of each cookie.

- Without hesitating, fold each cookie in half and press edges to seal.

- Fold warm cookie over the edge of a clean bowl and hold for approximately 20 seconds to set shape.

Let cookies cool and enjoy yummy cookies and wild FORTUNATELY/ UNFORTUNATELY stories together.

For activity on pages 120-121, 128-129, 144-145

Activity Planning Sheet

Activity:_____

Duty	Supplies Needed	Who's Responsibility	Date to Complete	Update	Check in/ Report

Examples of Codes

Number Substitutions:

1	2	3	4	5	6	7	8	9	10	11	12	13	14	15	16	17	18	19	20	21	22	23	24	25	26
a	b	c	d	e	f	g	h	i	j	k	l	m	n	o	p	q	r	s	t	u	v	w	x	y	z

You can change the order of the numbers and letter match so that maybe a = 4, r= 1 etc. to make the code harder to break.

You can do the same thing with letter substitutions.
For example: s y m b o l a c e d f g h i j z x w v q r t u p n k
             a b c d e f g h i j k l m n o p q r s t u v w x y z

The Polybius Square

Each letter can be referred to as a pair of numbers: 1,4 is a D. / is used to indicate an end to a word. For example, 2,3, 1,5, 3,2, 3,2, 3,5/ means "Hello." To make the code more complicated you can change the order of the letters, as long as both you and the person who gets the code has a key.

	1	2	3	4	5
1	A	B	C	D	E
2	F	G	H	I	J
3	K	L	M	N	O
4	P	Q	R	S	T
5	U	V	W	X	Y or Z

Book Codes

Both the writer and the receiver have to have the same book in order to use this code. Make sure the editions of the books are the same. Numbers are used to show the page of the book and the line on the page which a word is to be found. The first word of the sentence on the page and the line listed is the "message" word. Or you can make it more complex by also listing the number of the position of the word on the line. For example, 10 17 8 would be the word found on page 10, line 7, 8th word on the line.

Morse Code

A	.-	J	.---	S	...	0	-----	8	---..
B	-...	K	-.-	T	-	1	.----	9	----.
C	-.-.	L	.-..	U	..-	2	..---	Fullstop	.-.-.-
D	-..	M	--	V	...-	3	...--	Comma	--..--
E	.	N	-.	W	.---	4	....-	Query	..--..
F	..-.	O	---	X	-..-	5	.....		
G	--.	P	.--.	Y	-.--	6	-....		
H	....	Q	--.-	Z	--..	7	--...		
I	..	R	.-.						

Fun Literacy Activities for After-School Programs

Defending Your Life

Only write phrases in this outline, so you will not be tempted to "read" your talk.

I. Introduction: (for example: personal story, poem, quote)

II. Main Ideas: This is not true because

　　1.

　　2.

　　3.

　　　　1st idea: Older people may think _____ but it is not true because

　　　　_____

　　　　example:

　　　　example:

　　　　<u>Ending statement:</u>

　　　　2nd idea: Older people may also think _____, but it is not true because

　　　　_____

　　　　example:

　　　　example:

　　　　<u>Ending statement:</u>

　　　　3rd idea: Older people may also think _____, but it is not true because

　　　　_____

　　　　example:

　　　　example:

　　　　<u>Ending statement:</u>

　　Conclusion: What older people and teenagers can do to get along.

"I Am ..." Poem

#1. I am

#2. Nouns about which you have strong feelings. Each word starts with a capital letter.

#3. Write complete sentence about two things that you like.

#4. Nouns that describe what you like to see in other people; end with "are important to me." Capitalize each noun.

#5. A sentence containing a positive thought or feeling. It can tell something that you find acceptable in yourself.

#6.-#7. Sentences in which you show something negative in yourself or others, however the sentence must be showing that out of something BAD can come GOOD. Use the word "but" to link the bad and good.

#8.-#9.-#10. Short sentences relating something about which you have strong feelings—likes or dislikes. They do not have to relate to each other or to the previous lines you have written.

#11. End with "This is me" or "I am."

Remember the following: A **noun** is a person, place or thing.
Examples: friend, home, baseball, courage, fear, Chicago, enemy, reason, happiness

Poem Example:

I am

Daughter, Friend, Free
I love reading a good book and listening to music.
Honesty, Senses of Humor, Craziness are important to me.
Times to be quiet are necessary for my happiness.
When people are mean to each other, I want to get mad, but I try to control
myself so I am not mean either.
I love having fun.
I hate doing homework.
I enjoy talking to my friends.

This is me
by Danielle Green

(Format used by permission from Marsha Rogers. Her poetry website can be found at http://www.msrogers.com/ English2/poetry/30_days_of_poetry.htm)

Multicultural Games Tournament

Game Title: _____

Team Members:

_____

The countries where it is played and its origin:

_____

_____

The Object of the Game:

_____

The Rules:

1. _____

2. _____

3. _____

4. _____

5. _____

6. _____

7. _____

8. _____

List the equipment needed.

For activity on pages 140-141

Journal Prompts

Sentence beginnings to help me think about how I feel about myself

- One way I am different from everyone else is . . .
- Most people think I am . . .
- The time when someone made me feel special was . . . .
- My parents show me that they like me when . . . . .
- I feel encouraged when . . .
- I am important because . . .
- One thing I do better than anyone else is . . .
- Other people are important because . . .

Sentence beginnings to help me think about responsibility and taking chances

- I think that the teacher's responsibilities are to...
- When my mom is upset with me, I . . .
- One time, I was afraid to try something new . . .
- I tried something that I thought I could do and it . . .
- I feel safe asking for help because . . .

Sentence beginnings to help me think about how I get along with people

- When my friend and I disagree about what we want to do, I...
- If someone does not like something I do I would like them to . . .
- When I'm upset, I like my friend to . . .
- When my mother is angry at me for something, I would like her to...
- If I am afraid of something, I would like my friend to . . .

Sentence beginnings to help me think about how I make decisions

- Something I enjoy doing that others do not is . . .
- Once I had a problem that no one else could help me with. I . . .
- Some problems I have right now are
- If I could earn my own money, I would feel . . .
- The problem I solved on my own was . . . .
- Some decisions I made today were . . .
- Something about myself (besides my looks) that I would like to change is . . .

Sentence beginnings to help me think about hope and "right and wrong"

- When I get in trouble, I . . .
- The worst thing I ever did to anyone was . . .
- One time I did something that I knew I'd get in trouble for, but I did it anyway because . . .
- A place that is very special to me is . . .
- When I get discouraged, I make myself feel better by . . .
- If my friend stole something, I would . . .
- When I have to make hard decisions, I . . .
- Five of the most important things in my life are . . .

Prefixes & Suffixes

(for use with "Name That Junk" activity)

Combining Forms	Meaning	Examples
astro	star	astronomy
auto	self	autobiography
bio	life	biography
brevi	short, brief	abbreviate
chrono	time	chronometer
cosmo	world, universe	cosmological
denti, dent	tooth	dentifrice, dental
geo	earth	geology
hydro	water	hydroplane
macro	large	macrocosm
micro	small; magnifies small things	microcosm, microscope
multi	many	multiply
ped, pede, pedi	foot	pedal, centipede, pedicure
phobia	fear	claustrophobia
phon, phone	sound	phonics, telephone
photo	light	photograph
scope	look	telescope

Prefixes	Meaning	Example
ante-	before	antebellum
anti-	against	anti-aircraft
circum-	around	circumvent
ex-, e-	out of, from	exit, emit
extra-	beyond	extraordinary
fore-	front	forehead
inter-	among; between	intersect
intra-	within	intramural
mis-	wrong	misadvise, mislead
non-	no, not	nonintervention
post-	after	postoperative
pre-	before	preview
semi-	half	semiannual
sub-	under	submarine
super-sur-	above, over	superintendent, surpass
trans-	across, over	transfer
ultra-	beyond	ultrashort

Suffixes	Meaning	Examples
-an	having to do with; inhabitant	Shakespearean, European
-ary, -arium, -orium	place for, belonging to	military, aquarium, auditorium
-ent	one who	president
-ess	female	heiress
-est	superlative ending	warmest, smartest
-ful	full of	playful
-hood	state of being	neighborhood, childhood
-ish	like, tending toward	greenish, smallish
-ive	of or having to do with	sportive
-ize	cause to become or resemble	Americanize
-less	without	smokeless, meatless
-ment	act of or state of	bewilderment
-ous	full of	joyous
-sect	to cut	bisect

Making Books with Bindings

Materials:

eight sheets of 8.5 x 11 paper
book board or other heavy paper
construction paper
needles
thread
scissors
rubber cement
materials to decorate the cover: colored pencils, markers, pictures for collages etc.

Instructions:

1. Fold the paper in half to form a 16-page booklet measuring 8 1/2 x 5 1/2.

2. Thread a needle with 24 inches of heavy thread.

3. Beginning at one end of the folded paper's center crease, sew large stitches about 1 inch apart, leaving 2 inches of the thread hanging from the first needle hole.

4. When you reach the end of the crease, turn the booklet over. Now sew back, bringing the needle through the same holes on the other side of the book. When you are finished stitching the pages together, tie the two ends of your thread together on the outside of your booklet. Trim the ends.

5. Cut two 6 x 9 inch rectangles from cardboard.

6. Lay the cut pieces side by side, leaving a half inch space between them. Cover the center gap with packaging tape, attaching the cardboard pieces together making sure that you leave a space so that they can be shut.

7. Cut a piece of construction paper 15 x 20 inches. Fold the construction paper around the cardboard "cover" and glue it. Fold the ends in the inside of the cardboard.

8. Place the closed pages into the open cover, putting the center of the booklet, sewn edge in, at the center of the book cover's spine. Tape it in place. Repeat the process on the other side.

9. The first and last pages of your booklet are the endpapers. Glue the first page flat against the cover. After it dries, glue the last page to the other side of the book cover.

10. Decorate and personalize the cover.

Adapted from "Making Books with Children," by Donna Stone found on *The New Homemaker,* http://www.newhomemaker.com/hands/crafts/bookmaking.html

What's to Eat?

Recipe Name: _____

General Description of Dish:

Ingredients:

Directions:

Cost per Serving:

Nutritional Facts:

Background on the recipe:

Written by: _____

References for Books/Videos Listed in the Activities

Activities for 5-8 year olds

Bark Paper Activity
1. Beth Wilkinson, **Papermaking for Kids: Simple Steps to Handcrafted Paper.** Gibbs Smith Publisher, 1997

Character Cutouts Activity
1. Georgia Guback, **Luka's Quilt.** Greenwillow, 1994.
2. Juan Felipe Herrera, **Grandma and Me at the Flea.** Children's Books Press, 2002.
3. Amy Hest, **Jamaica Louise Jones.** Candlewick Press, 1997.
4. Patricia Polacco, **My Rotten Redheaded Older Brother.** Aladdin Library, 1998.
5. Arnold Lobel, **Frog and Toad are Friends.** Harper Collins, 1970.
6. David Shannon, **Bad Case of Stripes.** Scholastic Paperbacks, 1998.
7. Vera Williams, **A Chair for my Mother.** Scott Foresman, 1984.

Creature Features Activity
1. Ellen Doris, **Entomology (Real Kids, Real Science Books).** Thames and Hudson, 1993.
2. Angels Julivert, **Fascinating World of Ants.** Barrons Juvenile, 1991.
3. Laurence Mound, **Eyewitness: Insect.** DK Publishing, 2000.

How are we Feeling? Activity
1. Jamie Lee Curtis, **I'm Gonna Like Me: Letting Off a Little Self-Esteem.** Joanna Cotler Publishing, 2002.
2. Kate Dicamillo, **Because of Winn-Dixie.** Candlewick Press, 2001.

Hug a Tree Activity
Fiction
1. Dr. Seuss, **The Lorax.** Random House, 1971.
2. Doris Gove, **My Mother Talks to Trees.** Peachtree Publishers, 1999.
3. Kate Kiesler, **Old Elm Speak: Tree Poems.** Houghton Mifflin Co, 1998.
4. Linda Glaser, **Tanya's Big Green Dream.** Simon & Schuster, 1994.

Non-Fiction
1. Barbara Brenner, **The Tremendous Tree Book (Reading Rainbow Book).** Boyds Mills Pr, March 1998.
2. David Burne, **Tree (Eyewitness Books),** Knopf, 1988.
3. Diane Burns, **Trees, Leaves and Bark (Take Along Guide).** NorthWord Press, 1998.
4. Catherine Chambers, **Bark (Would You Believe It).** Raintree/Steck Vaughn, 1996.

5. Andrew Charman, **I Wonder Why Trees Have Leaves: and Other Questions about Plants.** Kingfisher Books, 1997.
6. Gail Gibbons, **Tell Me, Tree: All about Trees for Kids.** Little Brown & Co, 1st edition 2002.
7. Patricia Lauber, **Be a Friend to a Tree (Let's Read-and-Find Out, Stage 2).** Harper Collins Juvenile Books, Revised edition, 1994.
8. Edward Parker, **Forests for the Future (Protecting our Planet).** Raintree/Steck Vaughn, 1998.
9. Natalia Ramanova, **Once There Was a Tree.** BT Bound, 1999.

My Own Book Activity

1. Jane Bayer, **A, My Name is Alice.** E.P. Dutton, 1992.
2. Lois Ehlert, **Eating the Alphabet: Fruits and Vegetables from A to Z.** Red Wagon Board Books, 1996.
3. Lisa Campbell Ernst, **The Letters are Lost.** Puffin, 1999.
4. Muriel Feelings, **Jambo Means Hello: Swahili Alphabet Book.** Dial Books for Young Readers, 1992.
5. Tana Hoban, **26 Letters and 99 Cents.** Mulberry Books, 1995.
6. Woodleigh Marx Hubbard, **C is for Curious: An ABC of Feelings.** Chronicle Books, 1995.
7. Margaret Musgrove, **Ashanti to Zulu: African Traditions.** Puffin, 1992.
8. Jerry Pallotta, **The Dinosaur Alphabet Book.** BT Bound, 1999.
9. Jerry Pallotta, **The Icky Bug Alphabet Book.** Charlesbridge Publishing Company, 1990.
10. George Shannon, **Tomorrow's Alphabet.** Mulberry Books, 1999.
11. Alan Snow, **The Monster Book of ABC Sounds.** Puffin, 1994.

Name Poems: Acrostics Activity

1. Kevin Henkes, **Chrysanthemum.** Mulberry Books, 1996.

Paper Plate Puppet Show Activity

1. Cheryl Henson, **The Muppets Make Puppets! Book and Puppet Kit: How to Make Puppets out of All Kinds of Stuff Around Your House.** Workman Publishing Company.

Playing with Song Lyrics Activity

1. Nancy and John Cassidy, **KidsSong** Series (Comes with Cassettes). Klutz Inc.
2. Avery Hart, **Kids Make Music! Clapping and Tapping From Bach to Rock!** Williamson Publishing, 1993.
3. Bessie Jones, **Step It Down: Games, Plays, Songs and Stories from the Afro-American Heritage.** University of Georgia Press, 1987.
4. Jose-Luis Orozco, **De Colores & Other Latin American Folk Songs for Children.** E.P. Dutton, 1994.

5. Maryls Swinger, **Sing Through the Day: Eighty Songs for Children** (Comes with a CD emphasizes multicultural selections) Plough Publishing House, 1999.

Illustrated books based on songs
1. Mary Ann Haberman, **The Eensy-Weensy Spider.** Little, Brown & Co., 2000.
2. Minfong Ho, **Hush!: A Thai Lullaby.** Orchard Books, 1996.
3. John Langstaff, **Oh, A Hunting We Will Go.** BT Bound, 1999.
4. Raffi, **The Wheels on the Bus**. Crown Publisher, 1990.
5. Timms Taback**, There was an Old Lady who Swallowed a Fly.** Vikings Children's Press, 1997.
6. Jeanette Winter**, Follow the Drinking Gourd** (Great book for Black History Month). Knopf, 1992.

Story Board Activity
1. Bill Cosby, **The Meanest Thing to Say.** Cartwheel Books, 1997.
2. Juanita Havill, **Jamaica's Find.** Houghton Mifflin Co. 1987.
3. Loretta Lopez, **The Birthday Swap.** Lee and Low Books, 1999.
4. Charlotte Pomerantz, **The Outside Dog.** Bt Bound, 1999.
5. Peggy Rathmann, **Ruby the Copycat.** Scholastic Paperbacks, 1997.
6. Cynthia Rylant, **The Relatives Came.** Pearson Learning, 1993.
7. Vera Williams, **A Chair for my Mother.** Scott Foresman, 1984.

Throwing for a Word Activity
1. Donald Bear, Marcia Invernizzi, Shane Templeton, Francine Johnston, **Words their Way: Word Study for Phonic, Vocabulary, and Spelling Instruction.** Prentice Hall; 3rd edition 2000.
2. Wiley Blevins, **Phonics from A to Z.** Scholastic Professional Books, 1999.
3. Wiley Blevins, **Quick-and Easy Learning Games: Phonics.** Scholastic Trade, 1999.
4. Michelle Ramsey, **Phonics Games Kids Can't Resist.** Scholatic Professional Books, 2000.

Tongue Twisters Activity
1. Alvin Schwartz, **Busy Buzzing Bumblebees & Other Tongue Twisters (I Can Read book).** Harpercollins, Revised edition, 1992.
2. Sarah Albee, **Elmo's Tricky Tongue Twisters**. Golden Books Pub Co Inc, 1998.
3. Joseph Rosenbloom, **Giggle Fit: Tricky Tongue Twisters**. Sterling Publications, 2002.
4. Grace Kim, **She Sells Seashells: A Tongue Twister Story (Hello Reader, Level 3)**, Cartwheel Books, 1996.
5. Joanna Cole, **Six Sick Sheep: One Hundred One Tongue Twisters**. Beech Tree Books, 1993.

Activities for 9-10 year olds

Can You Save the Day? Activity

1. Alice Dalgliesh, **The Courage of Sarah Noble**. Simon & Schuster; 2nd edition, 1991.
2. Lar Desouza, **Boys who Rocked the World: From King Tut to Tiger Woods.** Beyond Words Publishing Co., 2001.
3. Gerald Hausman, **The Coyote Bead**. Hampton Roads Publishing Co., 1999.
4. Mary Hoffman, **Amazing Grace.** Scott Foresman, 1991.
5. Milly Lee, **Earthquake.** Francis Foster Books, 2001. .
6. Barbara Lewis, **Kids with Courage: True Stories about Young People Making a Difference**. Free Spirit Publishing, 1992.
7. Robert N. Munsch, **Paper Bag Princess**. Annick Press, 1988.

Clap Those Hands Activity

1. Sara Bernstein, **Hand Clap! "Miss Mary Mack" and 42 other Hand Clapping Games for Kids.** Adams Media Corporation, 1994.
2. Joanna Cole and Stephanie Calmenson, **Miss Mary Mack and other Children's Street Rhymes.** William Morrow & Co Paper, April 1990.

Word Pictures: Concrete Poetry Activity

1. Brad Burg, **Outside the Lines: Poetry at Play.** Putnam Pub Group, 2002.
2. Jane Bransfield Graham, **Splish, Splash.** BT Bound, 2001.
3. Paul B. Janeczko, **A Poke in the I.** Candlewick Press, 2001.
4. J. Patrick Lewis, **Doodle Dandies: Poems that Take Shape.** Aladdin Library, 2002.

Fairy Tale Characters on Trial Activity

1. Berlie Doherty, **Fairy Tales.** Candlewick Press, 2000.
2. Tara McCarthy, **Multicultural Fables and Fairy Tales.** Scholastic Paperbacks, 1999.
3. Marie Ponsot, **The Golden Book of Fairy Tales (Golden Classics).**
4. Jack Zipes, **Don't Bet on the Prince: Contemporary Feminist Fairy Tales in North America and England** Routledge Kegan & Paul, 1989.

Grab Bag Demonstrations: Beyond Show and Tell Activity

1. Susan Hood, **Show and Tell (Real Kids Readers).** Millbrook Press, 1999.
2. Steve Mandel, **Effective Presentation Skills: A Practical Guide for Better Speaking**. Crisps Publication, 3rd Edition, 2000.
3. Gary Souter, **Creating E-Reports and Online Presentations**. Enslow Publishers, Inc., 2003.

Fiction

1. Mike Reiss, **The Great Show and Tell Disaster.** Price Stern Sloan Publishing, 2001.

Movie Posters Activity

1. Lloyd Alexander, **The Fortune-Tellers.** Puffin, 1997.
2. Jerdine Nolen, **Raising Dragons.** Silver Whistle, 1998.
3. David Shannon, **Bad Case of Stripes.** Scholastic Paperbacks, 1998.
4. Gary Soto, **Chato's Kitchen.** Paper Star, 1997.
5. Colin Thompson, **How to Live Forever.** Knopf, 1996.
6. David Wisniewski, **Golem.** Clarion Books, 1996.

Pet Rocks Activity

1. Byrd Baylor, **Everybody Needs a Rock.** Scott Foresman, 1985.
2. Laura Evert, **Rocks, Fossils and Arrowheads (Take-Along Guide).** Northwood Press, 2001.
3. Sue Fuller and Christopher Maynard, **Backpack Books: 1, 001 Facts about Rocks & Minerals (Backpack Books).** Dorling Kindersley; 1st edition, 2002.
4. Cally Hall and Harry Taylor, **DK Handbooks: Rocks and Minerals.** Dk Publication Merchandise, 1st edition, 2000.
5. Chris Pellant, **Smithsonian Handbooks: Rocks & Minerals (Smithsonian Handbooks).** DL Publication Merchandise, 2002.
6. R. F. Symes, **Eyewitness: Rocks & Minerals.** DK Publishing; 1st edition, 2000.

Mail Call Activity

1. Melvin Berger and Gilda Berger, **Where Does the Mail Go?: A Book About the Postal System (Discovery Readers).** Ideals Children's Book, 1994.
2. Andrea Davis Pinkney, **Abraham Lincoln: Letters from a Slave Girl (Dear Mr. President)** Winslow Press, 2001.
3. Schim Schimmel, **Dear Children of the Earth: A Letter from Home.** NorthWord Press, May 1994.
4. Alex Stewart, **Sending a Letter (Everyday History).** Franklin Watts, Inc. , 2000.

Fiction

1. Soyung Pak, Susan Kathleen Hartung, **Dear Juno.** Viking Childrens Books, October 1999.

Reader's Theater Activity

1. Suzanne I. Barchers, **Readers Theatre for Beginning Readers,** Teacher Ideas Press, 1993.
2. Suzanne I. Barchers, Jennifer L. Kroll, **Classic Readers Theatre for Young Adults.** Libraries Unlimited, 2002.
3. Suzanne I. Barchers, **Fifty Fabulous Fables: Beginning Readers Theatre,** Teacher Ideas Press, 1998.
4. Suzanne I. Barchers, **Scary Readers Theater.** Teacher Ideas Press, 1994.
5. Suzanne I. Barchers, **Multicultural Folktales: Readers Theatre for Elementary Students.** Teacher Ideas Press, 2000.
6. Lisa Blau, **Super Science!: Reader's Theatre Scripts and Extended Activities.** One from the Heart, 1997.

7. Anthony D. Fredericks. **Frantic Frogs and Other Frankly Fractured Folktales for Readers Theatre.** Teacher Ideas Press, 1993.
8. Justin McCory Martin, **12 Fabulously Funny Fairy Tale Plays**. Scholastic Professional Books, 2002.
9. Carol Pugliano, Carol Pugliano-Martin. **Just-Right Plays: 25 Emergent Reader Plays Around the Year (Grades K-1).** Scholastic Paperbacks, 1999.

Riddle Book Activity

1. Joseph Rosenbloom, **Biggest Riddle Book in the World.** Sterling Publication, 1983.
2. Charles Keller, **Best Riddle Book Ever.** Sterling Publications, 1998.
3. Mike Artell, **Starry Skies: Questions, Facts and Riddles About the Universe.** Goodyear Publishing Co., 1997.
4. Exploratorium Staff, **The Brain Explorer.** Henry Holt & Co.; 1 edition 1999.

Secret Messages Activity

1. Richard Churchill et al, **365 Simple Science Experiments With Everyday Materials.** Black Dog & Leventhal Publishing, 1997.
2. Hy Kim, **Showy Science: Exciting Hand-On Activities that Explore the World Around Us.** Goodyear Publishing Co., 1994.
3. Pat Murphy et al, **The Science Explorer: Out and About.** Henry Holt, 1997.
4. Deborah Schecter, **ScienceArt: Projects and Activities that Teach Science Concepts and Develop Process Skills.** Scholastic Paperback, 1999.

Tissue Paper Stories Activity

Picture Books Illustrated with Tissue Paper Collages
Any book by Eric Carle

1. **Do You Want to Be My Friend?** Harper Collins Juvenile Books; Board edition, 1995.
2. **The Very Busy Spider.** Philomel Books; Board edition, 1995.
3. **The Grouchy Lady Bug.** Scott Foresman 1996.
4. **The Very Hungry Caterpillar.** Philomel Books; Board edition, 1994.
5. Marguerite Davol, Robert Sabuda, **The Paper Dragon.** Atheneum, 1997.

Paper Making and Illustrations

1. Helen Bliss and Ruth Thomson, **Paper (Craft Workshop, No.1).** Crabtree Publications, 1998.
2. Eric Carle, **You Can Make a Collage: A Very Simple How-To Book.** Kultz, Inc., 1998.

Treasure Hunt Activity

1. Lenny Hort, **Treasure Hunts! Treasure Hunts!** Harper Collins Publishers, 2000.

Fiction and non-fiction about treasure hunts

1. Jennifer Barrett, **The Seven Treasure Hunts.** HarperTrophy, 1992.
2. Judy Donnelly, **True-Life Treasure Hunts (Step into Reading, Step 4.)** Random House, 1993.

3. Jackie Gaff, **The Mummy: Treasure Hunt** ™ . Larousse Kingfisher Chambers, 2002.
4. Jahnna N. Malcolm, **The Sapphire Princess Hunts for Treasure (Jewel Kingdom , No 6).** Little Apple, 1998.
5. Donald J. Sobol, **Encyclopedia Brown and the Case of the Treasure Hunt.** Bantam Skylark; Reissue edition, 1989.

Write a Rap Activity

1. Marvin Terban, **Time to Rhyme: A Rhyming Dictionary.** Boyds Mills Pr., 1997.

Activities for 11-13 year olds

Book Soundtrack Activity

1. Robert Burleigh, **Hoops.** Harcourt Inc., 2001.
2. Eleanor Coerr, **Sadako and the Thousand Paper Cranes.** Puffin, 1999.
3. Julie Ann Peters, **Revenge of the Snob Squad.** Puffin, 2000
4. Maurice Sendak, **Where the Wild Things Are.** HarperCollins Publishers, 1963.
5. R.L. Stine, The **Goosebumps** series. (Varies. However, Scholastic Paperbacks publishes many of the books.)
6. Mildred Taylor, **The Gold Cadillac**. Dial Books for Young Readers, 1987.

Campaign for a Good Cause Activity

1. Barbara Lewis, **Kids with Courage**: True Stories about Young People making a **Difference,** Free Spirit Publishing, 1992.
2. Barbara A. Lewis, **The Kid's Guide to Social Action: How to Solve the Social Problems You Choose—and Turn Creative Thinking into Positive** Action (Revised, Expanded, Updated Edition). Free Spirit Publishing, 1998.
3. Barbara A. Lewis, **The Kid's Guide to Service Projects: Over 500 Service Ideas for Young People Who Want to Make a Difference.** Free Spirit Publishing, 1995.

Coded Messages Activity

Fiction

1. Lynne Barasch, **Radio Rescue**. Francis Foster Books, 2000.
2. Sara Hoagland Hunter, **The Unbreakable Code.** Northland Publishers, 1996.
3. Dana Meachen Rau and Bari Weissman, **The Secret Code** (Rookie Readers. Level C). Children's Press, 1998.
4. John Warner and Peggy Nicholson, **Case of the Mysterious Codes**. Lerner Publications Company, 1994.
5. Jeanette Winter, **Follow the Drinking Gourd.** Knopf, 1992.

Activities

1. Martin Gardner, **Codes, Ciphers and Secret Writing.** Dover Publications, 1984.
2. Helen Huckle, **The Secret Code Book.** Dial Books for Young Readers, 1995.

3. Jim Wiese, **Spy Science: 40 Secret-Sleuthing, Code-Cracking, Spy-Catching Activities for Kids.** John Wiley & Sons, 1996.
4. Video: **Look What I Found: Making Codes and Solving Mysteries,** Intervideo, Inc. 1993.

What's to Eat?: Making Cookbooks Activity
1. Arlette N. Braman, **Kids Around the World Cook!:** John Wiley & Sons, 2000.
2. Jennifer Dorland Darling, **Better Homes and Gardens New Junior Cookbook.** Meredith Books, 1997.
3. Evelyn Raab and George Walker, **Clueless in the Kitchen: A Cookbook for Teens.** Firefly Publications, 1998.
4. B. Weith and T. Harms. **Cook and Learn: Pictorial Single Portion Recipes: A Child's Cook Book.** Addison-Wesley Pub Co; 1981.

Presto, Magic Show Activity
Books
1. James Baker, **Illusions Illustrated: A Professional Magic Show for Young Performers.** Lerner Publication Company, 1988.
2. J.B Bobo, **Modern Coin Magic.** Dover Publications, 1982.
3. Karl Fulves, **Easy-To-Do Card Tricks for Children.** Dover Publications, 1990.
4. C.S Lewis, **A Guide for Using The Lion, The Witch and The Wardrobe in the Classroom.** Teacher Created Materials, 2000.
5. Fay Presto, **Magic for Kids.** Larousse Kingfisher Chambers, 1999.
6. Jim Wiese, **Magic Science: 50 Jaw-Dropping, Mind- Boggling, Head-Scratching Activities for Kids.** John Wiley & Sons, 1998.
Video
1. Michael Ammar, **Anytime, Anyplace Magic.** 1991.
2. Michael Ammar, **The Complete Introduction to Coin Magic,** 2000.
3. Val Valentino, **Magic's Biggest Secrets Finally Revealed!** E-Realbiz.com, 1998

Multicultural Game Tournament Activity
1. Lorraine Barbarash, **Multicultural Games.** Human Kinetics Publication, 1999.
2. Glen Kirchner, **Children's Games from Around the World.** Benjamin/Cummings, 2000.
3. Louise Orlando, **The Multicultural Game Book.** Scholastic Paperbacks, 1999.

Suggested Websites for Activities

(At the time of publication these web addresses were correct. If they no longer work, we are sorry. The nature of the web is ever changing.)

Section One: Activities for 5-8 year olds

Website for *Bark Paper* Activity
Directions for Making Paper: Very detailed directions on how to make new paper from old newspapers and other recycled paper stuff. http://www.tappi.org/paperu/art_class/makingPaper.htm

Website for *How are We Feeling?* Activity
Absolutely Whootie: Stories to Grow By, For more stories that are easy to act out. http://www.storiestogrowby.com/
Aesops Fables, http://www.portal5.co.uk/books/aesop/THE%20FABLES.txt

Websites for *Hug a Tree* Activity
Trees for Kids, http://www.treesforyou.org/Kids/kids.htm
Forest Puzzles: Links http://www.omsi.edu/visit/life/forestpuzzles/links.html

Website for *Name Poem* Activity
ProTeacher Page: What's in a Name? Great ideas for activities using children's names. http://www.proteacher.com/cgi-bin/outsidesite.cgi?external=http://www.geocities.com/Heart-land/Hollow/1213/names.html&original=http://www.proteacher.com/070084.shtml&title=Names%20Unit

Websites for *Paper Plate Puppet Show* Activity
Puppet making for kindergarteners: http://www.enchantedlearning.com/crafts/puppets/
Puppet Craft Projects: Links to descriptions of many different kinds of easily made puppets. http://craftsforkids.about.com/msubpuppet.htm?COB=home&terms=puppetry

Websites for *Playing with Music* Activity
Children's Music and Songs http://falcon.jmu.edu/%7Eramseyil/songs.htm
Children's Songs: http://www.theteachersguide.com/ChildrensSongs.htm

Website for *Tongue Twister* Activity
The Tongue Twister Database: http://www.geocities.com/Athens/8136/tonguetwisters.html
1st International Collection of Tongue Twister http://www.uebersetzung.at/twister/
Tongue Twisters for the ESL/EFL Classroom (Tongue twisters in alphabetical order) http://members.tripod.com/~ESL4Kids/tongue.html
The Children's Stomping Ground Tongue Twisters: http://www.oink.demon.co.uk/fun/tt/tonguet.htm

Tongue Twister Lesson Plan: http://www.lessonplanspage.com/
LAOTongueTwistersCollectionK6.htm

Alliteration Lesson Plans and Resources: (For upper elementary and middle school age) http://volweb.utk.edu/Schools/bedford/harrisms/1allitera.htm

Section Two: Activities for 9-10 year olds

Websites for *Fairy Tale Characters on Trial* Activity

Tales of Wonder: Folk and Fairy Tales from Around the World http://www.darsie.net/talesofwonder/

Myths, Fables, Fairy Tales and Folktales: Great links to traditional and multicultural stories. http://www.gomilpitas.com/homeschooling/explore/myths.htm

Script for "The True Story of the Three Little Pigs" by Jon Scieszka. http://members.aol.com/_ht_a/rcswallow/TruePigs.html?mtbrand=AOL_US

Websites for *Reader's Theater* Activity

Aaron Shepard's RT Page: The best website related to reader's theater. It has suggestions for staging and scripts. http://www.aaronshep.com/rt/

Reader's Theater Scripts and Plays: Many downloadable scripts written at various reading levels. http://www.teachingheart.net/readerstheater.htm

Readers Theater/Language Arts Home Page for Teachers by Rick Swallow: More Scripts. http://hometown.aol.com/rcswallow/

Free Scripts and Teacher's Guide: More scripts and simple instructions on how to perform them. http://loiswalker.com/catalog/guidesamples.html

Websites for *Riddle Books* Activity

Jokes and Riddles for Children: All types of riddles. http://www.brownielocks.com/jokes.html

Scatty.Com: Lots of riddles and jokes. Many pop-up screens however. http://www.scatty.com/index.html

Websites for *Tissue Paper Stories* Activity

Family Crafts: Printmaking Great website with all sorts of links to different kinds of easy print making ideas using common objects like combs, fruits and leaves. http://familycrafts.about.com/cs/printmaking/

Section Three : Activities for 11-14 year olds

Website for *Breaking the Code* Activity

Discovery School Puzzlemaker, http://puzzlemaker.school.discovery.com/cryptogramSetUpForm.html

Websites for *Writing Children's Books with a Message* Activity
List of books about Trauma and Loss: http://www.cbcbooks.org/html/cbc_booklist.html
Bibliotherapy and Children's Books: http://falcon.jmu.edu/~ramseyil/bibliotherapy.htm

Websites for *Crosswords and Word Searches* Activity
Discovery School: http://puzzlemaker.school.discovery.com/
Puzzles.com: http://www.puzzles.com/
Daily Word Searches: http://www.mirroreyes.com/wordsearch/

Websites for *Multicultural Games Tournament* Activity
Germantown Academy Multicultural Games: Great website the rules are written by young people. http://www.ga.k12.pa.us/Academics/MS/6th/MCGAMES/Directory.htm
International Games: The rules for some of the games are in both English and Spanish: http://www.gameskidsplay.net/games/foreign_indexes/index.htm
World Games: http://www.gamekids.com
Grid for Battle Ship Game: http://www.proteacher.com/cgi-bin/ outsidesite.cgi?external=http://www.funorama.com/images/battleships.gif&original=http:// www.proteacher.com/090030.shtml&title=Battleship

Website for What's to Eat?: Making Cookbooks
Welcome to Cooking with Young Children: http://members.aol.com/sgrmagnlia

Activities Index

Activity	Reproducible	Page

Fun Literacy Activities for After-School Programs

Notes

Notes

Fun Literacy Activities for After-School Programs